Contents

1

Introduction

In order to be able to claim compensation for harm caused by D's negligence, three things must be proved:

D owes C a duty of care

D breached that duty

D's breach caused the harm

You may have studied tort before, perhaps at AS level, however you need more depth to your knowledge for the higher level examinations. Not only are there new areas not covered elsewhere, but also there is more on breach of duty, in particular as regards medical negligence, and on duty and breach as regards product liability. The rules on causation are also covered in more depth to include successive and multiple causes and loss of chance.

The first chapter covers duty, breach and causation in relation to physical harm, including product liability and medical care. The following two chapters look at the special rules for proving duty in relation to economic loss, negligent misstatement and psychiatric harm (the rules for breach and causation are the same for all types of harm or loss which is why these are covered in the first chapter).

The tasks are intended to reinforce your learning so do these as you go along. There are plenty of tasks to help with applying the law. The answers are at the end of the book. One or two tasks will ask you to jot down a few thoughts for use in an essay question, so there are no answers to these, but keep your notes for revision and exam practice. I have included occasional quotes so use these too; they show that you know what judges have to say about the law. However, if you are studying for the AQA board of examinations you won't need to consider the problems or reforms as there are no evaluation questions in the AQA examination.

Examination tip

Establishing that a duty is owed is important because if there is no duty, the claim will fail. There will be no need to consider breach of that duty or causation. If a duty is established, the rules for breach and causation are the same for *all* negligence cases. It is only the rules on duty that differ, depending on the type of harm suffered, so make sure you understand these and the relevant cases.

The three types of harm which may be caused by another's negligence are:

Physical harm: Damage to a person or property

Economic harm: Financial loss

Psychiatric harm: Mental rather than physical harm

Examples

Some of you may have seen these cases before if you studied tort for AS.

In **Donoghue v Stevenson** a women suffered **physical** harm after consuming a drink containing a decomposed snail.

In **Caparo v Dickman** a purchaser of shares suffered **economic** loss having relied on information provided by auditors who had negligently prepared a company's accounts.

In **Bourhill v Young**, a pregnant woman suffered **psychiatric** harm having gone to the scene of a crash and seen blood on the road.

We'll look at these cases again as we come to the relevant area of law.

As mentioned above, each type of loss, or harm, has special rules for proving a duty of care and there is a chapter on each. The first chapter also includes breach and causation as these apply to all three types of harm.

"You must take reasonable care to avoid acts or omissions which you can reasonably foresee would be likely to injure your neighbour" - Lord Atkin

Duty of care for physical harm

Whether a duty is owed in relation to physical harm is based on what is known as the 'neighbour principle' from **Donoghue v Stevenson 1932.** This case is famous for establishing liability in negligence, and is often referred to as 'the snail in the ginger beer case'.

Mrs Donoghue was in a café with her friend. She drank some ginger beer with her ice cream, and later she emptied the rest of the contents into a glass. To her horror, a decomposing snail came out. She was ill (whether from drinking the beer or from seeing the snail in its state of decomposition is not clear) and sued the manufacturer. As her friend had paid, there was an important legal issue to consider. Mrs Donoghue was owed no duty under contract law because she did not buy the drink herself. The case eventually went to the HL on the issue of whether the manufacturer could owe a duty in tort to a consumer who did not buy the goods. Lord Atkin gave the leading judgment and produced the now famous 'neighbour test'. He said that the biblical requirement that we must 'love our neighbour' became, in law, that we must not injure our neighbour. He said, *"You must take reasonable care to avoid acts or omissions which you can reasonably foresee would be likely to injure your neighbour"*. He then goes on to answer the question 'who then, in law, is my neighbour?' and answers, *"persons who are so closely and directly affected by my act that I ought reasonably to have them in contemplation as being so affected when I am directing my mind to the acts or omissions which are called in question"*

So a precedent was set. Tort law now protects those without a contract.

Example

I am baby-sitting for someone at work and being paid. I have a contract so I owe a duty under the contract, and can be sued if the baby is harmed due to my negligence. However, if I am baby-sitting for free, perhaps for a friend, then there is no contract. Since **Donoghue v Stevenson**, I can be sued in tort, as I owe a duty to anyone affected by my acts or omissions. The baby would be someone I would have in mind when I am contemplating, or thinking about, doing, (or omitting to do), whatever is being questioned – my negligent action (or inaction).

The test is essentially one of foreseeability. If the result of your actions may foreseeably harm someone, you will owe that someone a duty of care.

Task 1

You may not be able to remember the entire quote so write out Lord Atkin's neighbour test in full, but then put it in your own words so it is clear to you.

Later judges began to use an incremental approach, i.e., not expanding in great leaps but bit by bit, case by case. A line from an Australian case has been quoted with much approval. The case is **Sutherland Shire County v Heyman 1985**, and the Judge, Brennan J, said,

"It is preferable, in my view, that the law should develop novel categories of negligence incrementally and by analogy with established categories."

In **Caparo v Dickman 1990**, these words were approved by the HL. The HL said that there was no general principle which applied to all cases and it was necessary to consider whether imposing a duty was 'just and reasonable' in the circumstances. A three-part test was established.

The Caparo test

For a duty to arise:

- there must be foreseeability of harm

- there must be proximity between C and D

- it must be fair, just and reasonable to impose a duty on D

Key case

In **Caparo v Dickman**, C had claimed that the auditors of a company's books owed him a duty of care. They had produced inaccurate accounts and he had lost money by investing in the company. Arguably, it was foreseeable that people in his position, who had relied on the accounts, would suffer loss. The HL held, however, that there was insufficient proximity between him and the auditors. The auditors produced the accounts for the company, to comply with the legal requirements to produce annual accounts, not for potential investors. Nor was it fair, just and reasonable to make the auditors liable for losses to unknown investors.

The first two parts of the **Caparo** test are similar to the neighbour test from **Donoghue v Stevenson**. The third is a matter of what is fair in the circumstances of the particular case.

In brief:

Caparo	Donoghue	Meaning
it must be foreseeable that someone will be harmed by D's actions	D should have that someone 'in contemplation' when acting	'someone' is a group, or class, of people not an individual. Thus a duty was owed to all consumers, not to Mrs Donoghue in particular. It is foreseeable that a consumer will be affected by the act or omission of a manufacturer.
there is proximity between C & D	C is D's 'neighbour'	there is some kind of legal connection or relationship between C & D
it is fair, just and reasonable to impose a duty on D	Not specifically mentioned, although it was arguably the attempt to achieve justice that extended the law	A matter of policy, of what is right in the circumstances

The **Caparo v Dickman** case involved economic loss rather than physical harm, but the 3-stage test applies to all types of harm. It is applied more strictly in relation to economic loss and psychiatric harm, and we will look at these the next two chapters. In **Caparo** itself, Lord Roskill recognised that *"there is no simple formula or touchstone"* for deciding whether to impose liability. The 3rd part of the test allows for a certain amount of flexibility, based on what is 'fair' in the circumstances.

Let's look at the three parts to the test.

Foreseeability

It must be foreseeable that D's act (or omission) could cause harm.

Example

In **Donoghue v Stevenson**, it was foreseeable that the manufacturer's act (of allowing a snail to get in the bottle), or omission, (the failure to clean the bottles properly), could harm a consumer of the ginger beer.

Despite Lord Atkin's words in **Donoghue v Stevenson** that you should avoid acts or omissions which *"you"* can foresee might injure your neighbour; the test for foreseeability is an objective one. It is what the *reasonable person* foresees, not what D foresees.

Proximity

The concepts of foreseeability and proximity overlap. The more proximate you are to someone, the more foreseeable it is that his or her actions may harm you. In **Bourhill v Young 1943**, a woman heard a motorcycle crash and went to the scene after the rider's body had been taken away. She saw blood on the road and claimed that the shock caused her to miscarry and lose her baby. She failed in her claim against the negligent driver, as she hadn't actually seen the accident. It was not *foreseeable* that she would be harmed nor was she in close *proximity* to the driver or the accident. It is not just physical proximity, however, but whether the *relationship* between the parties is proximate enough.

Examples

In **Donoghue v Stevenson**, the relationship was one between a manufacturer and consumers. In **Caparo v Dickman**, there was proximity of relationship between the auditors and the company whose accounts they did, but not between the auditors and investors. The latter relationship was not sufficiently close, or 'proximate'.

Fair, just and reasonable to impose a duty

This is a matter of public policy and is perhaps the most difficult of the three parts of the Caparo test. It means that the court looks at what is best for society as a whole and / or may restrict the duty to avoid 'opening the floodgates' to claims. Actions against public bodies such as the police, hospitals, rescue services and local councils may therefore fail on this point because these groups provide a public service (which is good for society) paid for from public funds (which would be seriously depleted if too many claims were made). This means that the courts may refuse to impose a duty on such groups, even though harm is foreseeable.

Key case

In **Hill v CC for West Yorkshire 1988**, a consequence of the 'Yorkshire ripper' case, the police were held not to owe a duty to potential victims of a crime after releasing a suspected killer through lack of evidence. When he killed again the mother of the victim sued the police, claiming they owed a duty to her daughter. The HL refused to find a duty, partly on lack of proximity between the police and an unknown member of the public. However, the policy issue also arose. The HL felt that the threat of being sued could make the police less efficient in carrying out their duties. This would not be in the public interest so it was not 'fair, just and reasonable' to impose a duty.

Immunity for the police is not, however, absolute. There have been several successful claims against the police where there has been a greater degree of proximity. This shows that all three parts of the test are connected. The more foreseeable something is, and the greater the degree of proximity, the more likely it is that it will be fair, just and reasonable to impose a duty. In **Reeves v MPC 1999**, the police were held to owe a duty to a prisoner who committed suicide whilst in their care and whom they knew to be a suicide risk. The police had left the door flap open and he used it to hang himself. An important factor in **Reeves** was that the police *knew* that he was a suicide risk. In another suicide case, **Orange v CC of West Yorkshire Police 2001**, a similar claim failed. In this case, the man who hanged himself while in custody, after being arrested whilst drunk, was *not* a known suicide risk.

In **Smith v CC of Sussex Police 2008**, (full name **Van Colle and another v CC of Hertfordshire Police; Smith v CC of Sussex Police 2008**, as it was a joint appeal), a claim was brought by the victim of a violent attack, who had told police about threats to him by his ex-partner. When the attack materialised he argued that the police owed him a duty to take reasonable steps to prevent the injury occurring. Harm was foreseeable, as the police knew about the threats and the whereabouts of the person from whom they came. The CA held that the police were liable. The HL considered the 'policy' element of the **Caparo** test, as applied in **Hill**, and noted that the 'core principle' of such cases was that imposing a duty would be detrimental to good policing, as it might make the police defensive and unwilling to take risks. The HL declined to move away from this principle and reversed the decision of the CA. No duty of care was owed.

In **Desmond v CC of Nottinghamshire Police 2011**, the CA confirmed that it was settled law that only in exceptional circumstances would it be in the public interest for police to owe individual members of the public a duty of care. This was because it was not usually in the interests of the whole community that, when carrying out their operational duties, the police should owe a duty to individuals. Exceptional circumstances could include times when there is greater foreseeability of harm and greater proximity between the police and the individual.

Example

Reeves v MPC can be used to illustrate all three parts of the test. Harm was *foreseeable* because the police knew that he was a suicide risk. There was *proximity* between C and the police because he was in one of the police cells. In such circumstances, it seems *fair, just and reasonable* to impose a duty on the police to the group of people – prisoners – who are in their care. There were no policy reasons to exclude a duty as it was to a limited, and known, group of people so would not be detrimental to policing generally. Also imposing a duty in these circumstances would not lead to a flood of claims as the duty would only be to prisoners in police care who were foreseeably at risk of harm.

Local councils also have some immunity from owing a duty of care. In **Sandhar v Department of Transport 2004**, C's husband had been killed when he skidded on ice on the road. The council had a policy in place in regard to salting the roads, but had not carried it out on this particular road. The court held that the council did not owe a duty to all road users to ensure that all roads were kept free of ice.

In **Gorringe v Calderdale MBC 2004**, C had been driving up a hill. Nearing the top she suddenly saw a bus coming towards her and she was injured when she hit it. She argued that there should have been a warning sign of some sort. The HL found that there was no duty to provide road signs. In **Fernquest v Swansea CC 2011**, a man sued the council after slipping on ice at a bus stop. The judge applied **Caparo v Dickman** and held that there was proximity between the parties and the risk of injury was foreseeable as the council knew about the ice. However, the CA reversed the decision and held that although injury was foreseeable, it was not fair, just and reasonable to impose a duty of care on a council for 'normal hazards' which members of the public could be expected to be aware of.

Again, as with the police, immunity is not absolute and the higher the risk of harm (foreseeability) the more likely a duty will be owed.

Example

In **Vernon Knight Associates v Cornwall CC 2013**, the CA held that a council owed a duty to local residents to keep drains clear to prevent flooding. It was therefore liable when it failed to do so. The council knew the risk of flooding during times of heavy rainfall and had previously taken steps to keep the drains clear. Flooding was highly foreseeable and there is a relationship between a council and local residents. It was therefore fair, just and reasonable to impose a duty of care on the council which they had breached by not keeping the drains clear on this occasion.

Sporting activities and certain types of entertainment are seen as for the public benefit so the courts may feel it is not 'fair, just and reasonable' to impose a duty on the people providing for such events. However, much depends on the circumstances and again the more foreseeable harm is, and the closer the relationship, the more likely it will be fair to impose a duty. In **Watson v British Boxing Board 2000**, the boxer Michael Watson suffered head injuries during a fight against Chris Eubank. He sued the Board on the basis that had proper medical treatment been given at the ringside he would not have suffered brain damage. The CA found that it was 'just and reasonable' to impose a duty on the Board to ensure adequate medical facilities were available, and upheld his claim. A similar decision was made in **Vowles v Evans 2003**, where a player was injured in an amateur rugby match when a scrum collapsed. Without going into the finer details of the rules of rugby, the essence was that the scrum collapsed due to the referee not applying the rules properly, and the player sued. Recognising that the rapport between referee and players is crucial to a good game of rugby, the court held that this would not be lessened by the knowledge that the referee owed a duty of care for the players' safety. Applying **Caparo v Dickman**, the CA held that as a matter of policy it is 'just and reasonable' that the law should impose a duty to take reasonable care for the players' safety. This could be achieved by the sensible and appropriate application of the laws of the game. **Vowles** can be compared to **Hill,** where it was thought police efficiency *would* be lessened by imposing a duty of care.

In **Everett & Harrison v Comojo 2011**, the CA applied the **Caparo** test to decide whether a nightclub owed a duty of care to its customers for the violent actions of a third party. A minor incident between the claimants and one of the waitresses led to a member of the club demanding an apology from the claimants. Later the member's driver arrived and the waitress was concerned by his manner. She went to tell the bar manager what had happened but in the meantime the driver stabbed the claimants several times. They sued the club's manager. The CA held that there was proximity between a nightclub and its customers, mainly because the club could regulate who entered, and there was also an economic relationship between a club and its customers. Harm was foreseeable because it is well known that consuming alcohol can lead to loss of control and violence. As regards whether it was fair, just and reasonable to impose a duty, the CA held that as there was a statutory duty under the **Occupier's Liability Act** to keep the premises safe, there was no reason the management should not also owe a duty at common law to keep customer's safe from third parties. In these circumstances it was fair, just and reasonable to impose a duty of care.

Finally in relation to a duty of care for physical harm or damage, we saw that in **Donoghue v Stevenson** it was established that a manufacturer owes a duty to a consumer in tort. This area of law is now governed by statute and has special rules.

Product liability

At common law, the consumer is afforded some protection by the tort of negligence as established in **Donoghue v Stevenson.** This law still applies, however the strongest legal weapon that a consumer has now is the **Consumer Protection Act 1987 (CPA)**. This makes a producer liable to all consumers for defective products.

The **CPA** is better than suing in tort as there is no need to prove a duty, merely that the defendant is a 'producer'. In addition, the **CPA** introduces strict liability, so the consumer need not prove fault, or breach of duty, when claiming for damage caused by defective or unsafe products. Finally, the Act gives greater protection to the consumer because if the seller has gone out of business, it may be possible to claim against the manufacturer, supplier or importer.

Example

Bjorn is at a friend's house and is injured when the microwave malfunctions. It was sold to his friend by Smith's Electrics, which has since gone out of business. Bjorn cannot sue in contract because, as in **Donoghue v Stevenson**, he did not buy the product and he cannot sue the shop because it has gone out of business. Instead Bjorn can sue the manufacturer of the microwave under the CPA.

There are three things to prove

   D is the producer of a product

   The product is defective

   The defect caused damage

D is the producer of a product

Under **s 1 (2)**, products include all goods which have been manufactured or processed. Since 2000, when an EU Directive brought crops into the definition of products, this includes agricultural crops.

Also under **s 1 (2)** and further explained in **s 2** 'producer' includes:

> *the manufacturer, abstractor (e.g., someone mining the product) and the processor (someone bottling, cooking or otherwise changing the product) of the product s 1 (2)*

> *a person who puts his name on the product thus holding himself out to be the manufacturer (e.g. supermarket own-brand goods) s 2 (2)(b)*

> *an importer into the European Union s 2 (2)(c)*

> *a supplier who will not respond to a request to identify the producer S 2 (3)*

The product is defective

The Act applies to defective rather than damaged goods, i.e. ones that are unsafe.

S 3 (1) defines a defect as being present when *"the safety of the product is not such as persons generally are entitled to expect"*. Under **s 3 (2)** this is assessed in regard to the circumstances and the court will take into account:

> *the advertising and marketing of the product*

> *any warnings or instructions as to use*

> *what might be reasonably expected to be done with the product*

> *the time when the product was supplied*

In **Bogle v McDonalds' Restaurants 2002**, a group of claimants sued McDonalds after being scalded by coffee and other hot drinks. They argued that McDonalds should have served the drinks at a lower temperature. The court held that the safety of the product met the public's expectations as to safety generally, as people generally expected hot coffee. McDonalds was not in breach of the **1987 Act**.

Example

We can see how the Act works by breaking down the above case.

Coffee is clearly a product under **s 1 (2)**. McDonalds was a producer under **s 1 (2)** as they had processed the coffee. The claim failed under **s 3 (1)** which defines a defect as being present when *"the safety of the product is not such as persons generally are entitled to expect"*. Under **s 3 (2)** this is assessed in regard to the circumstances and among other things the court will take into account what might be reasonably expected to be done with the product. As most people will expect to drink hot coffee **s 3** is not satisfied and the claim fails.

Other case examples

In **Richardson v LRC Products Ltd 2000**, a producer of condoms was not liable when one did not prevent a pregnancy, as people know that condoms are not fully effective in doing so.

In contrast, in **A v National Blood Authority 2001** several people became infected with hepatitis following blood transfusions. The contaminated blood provided by the Authority was held to be a defective product because people generally expect blood to be safe.

In **Tesco Stores Ltd v Pollard 2006**, a young child opened a bottle of dishwasher powder that was said to be child-resistant, and ate some of the powder. At trial it was held that the top was defective as it had been marketed as being child-resistant and people generally were entitled to expect the cap to conform to the relevant British Standard. On appeal the CA reversed the decision and held that people were entitled to expect that the bottle would be more difficult to open than an ordinary screw top bottle, but not necessarily to expect it to conform to a voluntary British Standard of which they were unaware. As the cap was more difficult to open than an ordinary screw top the product was not defective.

In **Abouzaid v Mothercare 2000**, a child was injured due to a faulty strap on his younger brother's pushchair. The CA held that people generally were entitled to expect more of Mothercare and held the manufacturer liable.

Finally, a case brought before the **CPA** but which would now fall under the **Act**. In **Grant v Australian Knitting Mills 1935**, a man had bought some underpants and contracted a skin disease due to a chemical in the material. In deciding the manufacturer owed him a duty of care the court followed the ratio of **Donoghue v Stevenson**. However, the underpants were clearly defective within the meaning of the **CPA** because people generally would not expect them to cause a skin disease. The court had also made clear that liability was partly due to the fact that the underpants were made for the purpose of being worn in the way that C had worn them. This would fall within **s 3(2)**, as regards what might be reasonably expected to be done with the product (wearing them).

Negligence (under **Donoghue/Caparo**) and the **CPA** overlap, although for the negligence C must prove a breach of duty not just that a product is defective.

Example

Grant v Australian Knitting Mills illustrates this overlap. In negligence a manufacturer owes a duty to a consumer because a consumer is someone likely to be affected by a manufacturer's act or omission (a 'neighbour'). This is the same under the **CPA**; a person wearing a manufacturer's products is someone likely to be affected by the manufacturer's actions (producing the underwear), and this means the manufacturer owes a duty of care to that person. Australian Knitting Mills were manufacturers (of underpants) and owed a duty to consumers of their products, (i.e., those that use the products, in this case Mr Grant who used the underpants). The product was defective in **Grant** because people generally would not expect underpants to cause a skin disease. The product was also defective in **Donoghue v Stevenson** as people generally would not expect snails in their ginger beer. The difference between the two actions is that in negligence a manufacturer is liable for negligent acts or omissions but negligence (breach of duty) must be proved. Under the **CPA** the manufacturer is liable only for defective goods, which means unsafe rather than merely faulty so is narrower, but no negligence need be proved so a claim is easier for C. A similarity between these cases is that the court was influenced by the fact that the defect could not reasonably be discovered. In **Donoghue v Stevenson** the bottles were opaque so the defect (the snail) could not be discovered by examination (by the cafe or the consumer). In **Grant** the chemicals were not visible so could not be discovered either by the shop that sold them or by the wearer, Mr Grant.

The defect caused damage

The normal causation rules apply as regards whether the defective product caused the damage. However damage is slightly more limited under the Act and covers:

> **Death or personal injury**
>
> **Loss of, or damage to, private property, but not business property, exceeding £275**

So you cannot claim for loss or damage to business property, nor any loss or damage to private property which is less than £275.

Defences

It is a defence under s4 to show any of the following:

> *The defect was attributable to a statutory requirement s4(1)(a)*
>
> *The product was not supplied to another s4(1)(b)*
>
> *The product was not supplied in the course of business s4(1)(c)*
>
> *The defect did not exist when the product was supplied s4(1)(d)*
>
> *The state of scientific and technical knowledge at the relevant time was such that the defect could not have been discovered s 4(1)(e)*
>
> *The defective product was comprised in another and the defect was wholly attributable to the design of the latter product*

The most commonly seen of these is the defence under **s 4(1)(e)**, known as the 'development risks' defence.

Examples

In **Roe v Ministry of Health 1954,** tiny cracks in a syringe led to contamination of an anaesthetic which left C paralysed. The state of scientific and medical knowledge at the time was such that this defect could not have been discovered, so the negligence claim failed on the fact that there was no breach of duty. If such a case were brought under the **CPA,** there would be no need to prove breach as the producer is strictly liable. However, the manufacturer or producer of the syringes would have a defence under **s 4(1)(e)** if sued because the state of scientific knowledge at the time was such that the defect could not have been discovered.

In **A v National Blood Authority** above, the judge held that the defence was not available because the possible risk of infection was known at the time.

In **Abouzaid v Mothercare 2000,** the CA held that the defence was not available because although it had not happened before, it was a risk that *could* have been discovered.

The defence of contributory negligence also applies, so that if the harm is partly caused by C's own negligence any award of damages may be reduced accordingly. This is governed by the **Law Reform (Contributory Negligence) Act 1945. S 1(1)** of the Act allows the court to use its discretion to reduce the damages awarded, *"to such extent as the court thinks just and equitable having regard to the claimant's share in the responsibility for the damage".*

Although not strictly a defence, any term attempting to exclude liability under the Act will be ineffective.

Task 2

Read the **Donoghue v Stevenson** case and answer the following questions.

> *Why couldn't Mrs Donoghue sue the shopkeeper?*
>
> *Whom did she sue and what did the HL decide?*
>
> *What might be a better course of action for her now, and why?*
>
> *How would this alternative course of action apply to the facts of Donoghue?*

Omissions

In **Donoghue v Stevenson**, Lord Atkin referred to *"acts or omissions"*. This means D can be liable for *not* doing something, as well as doing something negligently. Liability for an omission occurs when there is a particularly close relationship, such as that between an employer and employee. There will also be liability where there is a high degree of control by one person over another; there will be a duty to take care of that person's safety, so that failure to do so may result in liability. An example is omitting to take care to prevent the man's suicide in **Reeves v MPC**.

Where there is a risk of harm and that risk was created, or known about, by D there is a duty to take steps to avoid it harming anyone, so that omitting to do so can result in liability. This is true even if the danger has actually been created by a third party, as long as D knew of it.

Example

In **Smith v Littlewoods 1987**, an owner of a disused cinema had left his property unsecured and vandals broke in. They caused a fire which spread to a neighbour's property. The omission here was not locking up the disused building properly. The neighbour sued the cinema owner on the basis that this omission had caused the fire damage. The claim failed because the owner had no idea that vandals had broken in so harm was not foreseeable. However, had the owner known of the vandals he would have been obliged to take action to prevent harm to others. The claim also failed on the issue of causation (D successfully argued that the act of the vandals had broken the chain of causation between the omission to secure the building and the fire) but the case illustrates the point that it is possible to have liability for an omission as well for an act.

You can see from this case that the issue of omissions connects with foreseeability. If D had known of the vandals breaking into the cinema then the damage would be more foreseeable and so a greater obligation to take care would arise. However the court made clear that a property owner is not expected to put a 24-hour guard on the property to ensure nobody enters it and creates a risk of damage to neighbouring property.

Examination tip

Note the words of Brennan J. He said that the courts should develop *novel* categories of negligence incrementally and by analogy with established categories. This means that you only need to use the 3-part test where it is a new situation and has not been in court before. An examiner may use a scenario where there is a clear duty because you are expected to focus on another issue, like breach or causation or the **Consumer Protection Act**. In this event, use the case where there was a duty to explain there will be one, and move on to the other issues.

Example

It has already been established, in **Donoghue v Stevenson**, that a manufacturer owes a duty to a consumer so this is not a 'novel' situation. If you have a scenario involving a manufacturer and consumer you can use **Donoghue** to say there will be a duty and then move on to breach or causation or the **Consumer Protection Act** as appropriate.

Summary of duty

Donoghue v Stevenson - the neighbour test on foreseeability

Caparo v Dickman - the 3-part test

> *Foreseeability (the possibility of D's actions causing harm to C)*
>
> *Proximity (a relationship between D & C - the parties to the action)*
>
> *Whether it is fair, just and reasonable to impose a duty. (Based on what is good for society and whether there should be immunity for, e.g., the police or a local council, and also whether imposing a duty of care will open the floodgates to other claims)*

Summary of product liability

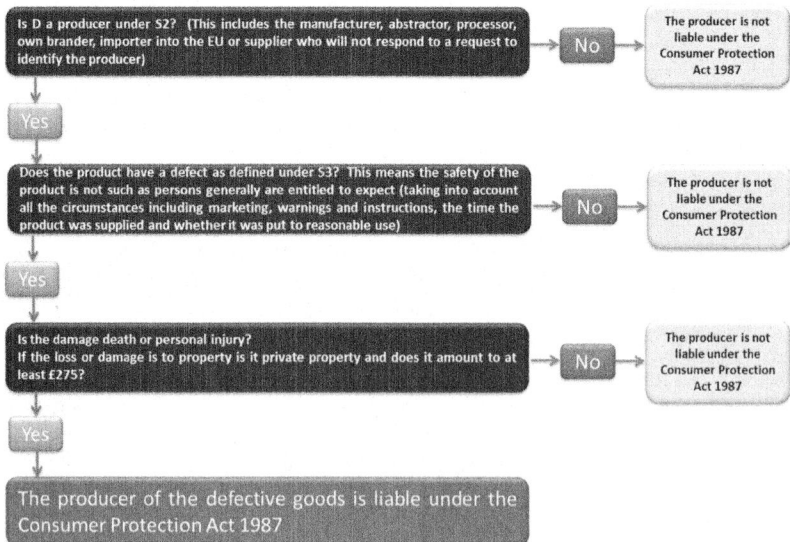

Is D a producer under S2? (This includes the manufacturer, abstractor, processor, own brander, importer into the EU or supplier who will not respond to a request to identify the producer) → **No** → The producer is not liable under the Consumer Protection Act 1987

Yes ↓

Does the product have a defect as defined under S3? This means the safety of the product is not such as persons generally are entitled to expect (taking into account all the circumstances including marketing, warnings and instructions, the time the product was supplied and whether it was put to reasonable use) → **No** → The producer is not liable under the Consumer Protection Act 1987

Yes ↓

Is the damage death or personal injury? If the loss or damage is to property is it private property and does it amount to at least £275? → **No** → The producer is not liable under the Consumer Protection Act 1987

Yes ↓

The producer of the defective goods is liable under the Consumer Protection Act 1987

| Do any of the defences apply? | → Yes → | The producer is not liable under the Consumer Protection Act 1987 |

↓ No

| The producer of the defective goods is liable under the Consumer Protection Act 1987 |

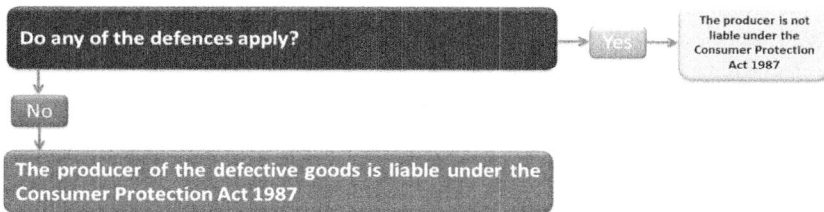

Examination tip

If there is a scenario involving faulty goods discuss the **CPA** first. If there is no liability under the **CPA** then go on to discuss negligence under the rules in **Donoghue v Stevenson** and **Caparo v Dickman** as an alternative.

Self-test Questions on duty

*What did Brennan J say in **Sutherland Shire County v Heyman**?*

*What is the 3-part **Caparo** test?*

Who might be immune from owing a duty?

*Why was there no duty in **Bourhill v Young**?*

*Why was no duty owed in **Caparo**?*

Breach of duty

"We must not look at the 1947 accident with 1954 spectacles" - Denning LJ

A breach of duty occurs when D has not taken care, i.e., has been negligent. To decide this, an objective test is used. The courts will consider what a reasonable person would have done given the same circumstances. In **Blyth v Birmingham Waterworks Co. 1856**, Baron Alderson said:

"Negligence is the omission to do something which a reasonable man...... would do, or doing something which a prudent and reasonable man would not do."

The reasonable person is a person in the particular set of circumstances that D is in.

Examples

We saw in **Vowles v Evans 2002**, that a referee in an amateur rugby match owed a duty of care for the players' safety. By allowing an inexperienced player to play in a scrum position for which he was not trained the referee was in breach of his duty. He hadn't reached the standard expected of a reasonable person in those circumstances, i.e., *a reasonable referee*.

In **Harris v Perry 2008**, a couple hired a bouncy castle for a birthday party and a boy was seriously injured by another child while playing on it. The judge held the couple had breached their duty of care by not supervising the children at all times. There was a higher risk of harm because children of different ages, and sizes, were playing together. The CA reversed the decision and held the standard of care required was that of a *reasonably careful parent*. In the circumstances a reasonably careful parent would have acted in the same way so they had reached the required standard. The CA noted that it was impossible to avoid all risk that children might injure themselves or each other when playing together.

In **Daw v Intel Corp (UK) Ltd 2007**, an employer knew an employee was suffering from severe stress but did little to remedy the situation. The CA upheld the decision that help had not been adequately provided so the employer had not reached the standard expected of a *reasonable employer* and was in breach of duty. The CA also restated the factors which apply in establishing breach and said an employer is only in breach of duty if there is a failure to take the steps which are reasonable in the circumstances, bearing in mind the magnitude of the risk of harm occurring, the gravity of the harm which may occur, the costs and practicability of preventing it, and the justifications for taking the risk.

As was restated by the CA in **Daw**, there are four main factors which are taken into account when deciding what a reasonable person would do, these are:

the magnitude of risk

the gravity of the potential harm

whether the risk was justifiable

the expense and practicality of taking precautions

Examination tip

Make sure you understand how the each of the factors apply, and learn at least a case on each. The more cases you know the easier it is to see what is needed when considering an examination scenario. The factors are balanced against each other in deciding whether D has done what is reasonable in the circumstances.

The magnitude or degree of risk

The greater the risk of harm, the greater is the obligation on D to take precautions. On the other hand, no breach will have occurred if the risk was impossible to foresee.

Example

In **Fardon v Harcourt-Rivington 1932**, D's car was parked on a street with a dog inside. As C walked past the dog jumped up and broke the window and some glass went in C's eye. There was no breach because the risk was impossible to foresee. The HL held there was no duty to guard against "fantastic possibilities".

In **Roe v Ministry of Health 1954**, contamination of an anaesthetic left C paralysed. Medical knowledge at the time was not such that this could have been expected; in fact it was this event that alerted the medical profession to the problem. There was no known, or foreseeable, risk, so the Ministry of Health was not liable. The court will not use hindsight to assess this. In **Roe**, Denning LJ made the comment opening this section on breach. It is whether the risk of harm was foreseeable *at the time*. This was seen again in **Maguire v Harland & Wolff plc 2005**. C's husband was exposed to asbestos dust at work, but he did not become ill, *she* did. She claimed damages on the basis that she was exposed to the dust he brought home. The judge found in her favour, saying that it was reasonably foreseeable that there was a serious risk to her health. The CA allowed D's appeal. At the time of C's exposure, the risks of secondary exposure were unknown. The injury to a member of C's family was therefore not foreseeable. Similarly in **Williams v University of Birmingham 2011**, a physics student who had been exposed to low levels of asbestos over 30 years before he became ill, sued the University. The CA held that the lack of knowledge of the dangers of exposure to small amounts of asbestos at the time meant the University had not breached its duty.

This shows that where the magnitude of risk is low there is unlikely to be a breach. In **Blair-Ford v CRS Adventures Ltd 2012**, C took part in a 'welly-wanging' contest at an activity centre. He was throwing a wellington boot backwards between his legs when he overbalanced and broke his neck. He sued for compensation. The judge ruled that it was a freak and tragic accident and rejected his claim.

In **Uren v Corporate Leisure 2013**, a man who was injured during a game at an RAF base sued the organisers of the game and the Ministry of Defence in negligence. The game involved running to an inflatable pool and then getting over the side to retrieve a piece of fruit floating in the water. C dived in head first and broke his neck. He argued that as the water was shallow going in head-first should have been prohibited. The court found that although there was some risk of harm from such an activity it was very small, and the existence of such a very small risk along with the fact there was some social value to outdoor activities, meant there was no breach of duty. This seems similar to **Blair-Ford v CRS Adventures Ltd**, however after an appeal a retrial was ordered and the decision reversed, this time the court said the harm more than minimally foreseeable and D should have taken precautions to avoid it.

If the risk is foreseeable, but small, the other factors may be relevant in deciding whether D had done enough. In **Bolton v Stone 1951**, a woman was hit by a cricket ball whilst walking near a cricket ground. The cricket club had taken precautions by erecting a 17-foot fence and the ball had gone over it only a matter of 5or 6 times in some 35 years. There was thus a foreseeable, but only very small, risk of a ball going over and, balanced against the other factors, the club had done all that was expected of it.

the gravity of the potential harm

A higher standard of care may be required where, although the *risk* is small, the *consequences* may be serious. This can be seen in **Paris v Stepney BC 1951**, where C was a worker who was already blind in one eye. Whilst doing some welding he was injured in the other eye. His job only involved a slight risk of injury, but the HL held that although a failure to provide goggles would not always make the council liable to their employees, in this case the seriousness of the harm that *could* occur was very great, because he was already blind in one eye. There was therefore a duty to take greater care.

Examination tip

The **Paris** case shows that a greater duty is owed to those suffering under a disability. This would also apply to children or the elderly, so look for clues in the scenario. What may be doing enough in respect of a fully able person may not be so in other cases. Note also that it is *potential* harm that is looked at. Don't be tempted to say that there is a breach because the harm actually suffered is very great. It is what harm *might* occur that is relevant, not what *has* occurred. This was confirmed in **Daw v Intel Corp (UK) Ltd** where the CA referred to the gravity of the harm "which may occur".

whether the risk was justifiable

The taking of a risk may be justifiable in certain circumstances. A risk which is of some benefit to society, for example, may be deemed acceptable even though it could be foreseen. In **Watt v Hertfordshire CC 1954**, a fireman was injured when a heavy car jack fell on him. The vehicle he was in was not adapted to carry such equipment, but it was held that this was an acceptable risk in the circumstances because they were on their way to rescue a woman trapped under a car.

Many sports and games have a social benefit which may make a risk of harm justifiable. However, risk-taking for the sake of it will not be acceptable even where there is a social benefit.

In **The Scout Association v Mark Barnes 2010**, the CA considered several breach factors in assessing whether the Association had breached its duty of care by allowing a game to be played with minimal lighting. The game involved running around and grabbing an object in the dark. The main lights were off but the emergency lighting was on and therefore there was some light. When a boy collided with a bench he injured his shoulder and sued. The trial judge found the Association had breached its duty of care and they appealed. On appeal the CA held that, balancing the risk of injury, the foreseeability of harm, the cost of preventing harm and the social benefit of the activity, there was a breach. The CA said that it was not the function of the law of tort to eliminate all risks but that the social value was limited and excitement for the sake of it did not justify the risk of harm.

Note also the **Compensation Act 2006 s 1**. This provides that in deciding whether D should have taken particular steps to meet the standard of care (e.g., take precautions) a court may consider whether a requirement to take those steps might prevent a desirable activity from being undertaken or discourage people from undertaking functions in connection with a desirable activity. This means a risk of harm may be justifiable when the activity in question is desirable, such as school trips and sporting events.

the expense and practicality of taking precautions

D may argue that avoiding a risk altogether would be too costly. The courts are unlikely to accept risk-taking based *solely* on the cost of avoidance, but it may tip the balance when considering the other factors. In **Latimer v AEC 1952**, the HL found a factory owner not liable for the injury to an employee who slipped on a wet floor. It was wet due to exceptional rain and flooding, and the owners had put down sand and taken other precautions. On the facts they had done enough. Shutting the factory would not only have been costly, but also impractical.

Examples

If everyone drove at 5 m.p.h. there would be fewer road accidents, but no one would expect the government to rule that such precautions should be taken. That would be impractical. In **Bolton v Stone**, the cricket club had already built a high fence – arguably, it would be impractical to do more than they had done, as in **Latimer v AEC**. By comparison, in **Paris v Stepney BC**, it would have been neither costly nor impractical to provide goggles.

Harris v Perry 2008 illustrates several factors. There was a high risk of harm because children of different ages, and sizes, were playing together. However, in considering what precautions should reasonably have been taken to protect against the risk of harm the CA held that it was impractical for parents to keep children under constant surveillance or supervision and it was impossible to avoid all risk that children might injure themselves or each other when playing together. Finally, the CA held that it would not be in the public interest to impose a duty upon them to do take further precautions against any risk of harm. In deciding they were not in breach the CA referred to the incident as *"a freak and tragic accident"*.

In **Uren v Corporate Leisure 2013**, discussed above, the court held that even though the risk was small and there was some social benefit, more precautions should have been taken such as banning diving head first. This can be compared to **Bolton v Stone** and shows how the factors are balanced against each other.

As was restated in **Daw v Intel Corp (UK) Ltd** the factors which help decide what is reasonable in the circumstances are the magnitude of the risk of harm occurring, the gravity of the harm which may occur, the costs and practicability of preventing it, and the justifications for taking the risk.

Examination tip

It is important to understand that these factors are balanced against each other and no particular factor will lead to a finding of breach alone. Look for particular clues in the given scenario so that you pick the relevant factors and the most appropriate case to use in support of your arguments. It may be that you need to discuss all four if the facts indicate all may be relevant.

Example

Using **Bolton v Stone 1951** we can say that the *potential harm* would be serious as cricket balls are very hard and could kill. However, this is balanced against the low *degree of risk* (it had rarely happened) and the *precautions* the cricket club had taken (erecting a high fence). It is also arguable that it was *justifiable* due to the social benefit of the game of cricket. On balancing these factors we can see that the club had done all that a reasonable club would do.

Objectiveness, children and professionals

The standard expected is said to be objective. It is based on what the reasonable person would do. A striking illustration of this is **Nettleship v Weston 1971**. Here a learner driver was liable for injuries to her driving instructor due to her negligent driving. The CA said that a learner driver should show the skill of an ordinary, competent driver.

However, the standard is also is measured by reference to the particular circumstances. Thus it is the standard expected of a reasonable parent, employer etc., as we saw earlier. This makes it slightly more subjective. This is particularly relevant in relation to children (of whom a lower standard is expected) and professionals (of whom a higher standard is expected). A child would be expected to reach the standard of a child of similar age, not an adult.

Example

In **Mullin v Richards 1998**, a schoolgirl of 15 was injured during a play-fight with another girl, using plastic rulers as swords. The CA found the other girl not to be liable in negligence. The point here was that although an adult may have seen the risk; a child would not.

In **Orchard v Lee 2009**, two boys had injured a playground supervisor whilst playing tag. Both were 13-years-old and the judge followed **Mullins v Richards** and held that the test was whether a 'prudent and reasonable' 13-year-old would have expected any injury to occur from his actions. The CA agreed and held that the primary question was whether their conduct had fallen below the standard that should objectively be expected of a reasonable child of that age. In the circumstance, they had been playing in an authorised play area and not breaking any rules. This was a simple accident and there was no liability in negligence.

In **Palmer v Cornwall CC 2009**, a claim was brought in respect of another incident which occurred during play-time at a school. A boy of 14 hit another boy in the eye while throwing stones at seagulls. The play area was supervised by dinner ladies and at the time only one was one duty. The victim's claim was rejected at trial but the CA reversed the decision and held that only one supervisor for around 300 children was clearly inadequate. If better supervision had been provided the boys may not have been throwing stones because they knew this was against the school rules. This time the claim succeeded, but this may be because it was brought against the council and not the other boy. Had the claim been against the other boy it may well have failed on the basis of **Mullin**, as was the case in **Orchard v Lee**.

Where D acts in a professional capacity the standard expected is that of a person in that line of work. This is often seen in cases of medical negligence.

Medical negligence

In medical cases the courts consider what is known as the '**Bolam** principle' established in **Bolam v Friern HMC 1957** and modified by the case of **Bolitho v City & Hackney HA**. This principle is used to assess whether errors of judgment by a doctor should be actionable in tort.

In **Bolam**, it was accepted that if a doctor acted in accordance with "a practice accepted as proper by a reasonable body of medical men" there would be no breach and therefore no liability.

Example

A doctor is examining a patient and fails to notice an abnormality which later leads to the patient developing cancer. Whether this error of judgment is a breach of the doctor's duty of care to the patient will depend on whether other doctors would have taken more care. If the doctor acted in the same way as other doctors would have done this will be seen as acting in accordance with 'a practice accepted as proper by a reasonable body of medical men' and the doctor will not be in breach.

The **Bolam** principle was modified slightly in **Bolitho v City & Hackney HA 1998**, where the HL added that the medical opinion must have some logical basis. Thus a doctor must show the skill that would be normal practice according to reasonable medical opinion i.e., what a reasonable body of medical men (and women) would expect of a doctor, not just any 'reasonable person', plus that medical opinion must have a logical basis.

In **Bolitho**, a doctor failed to attend promptly to a patient and the patient subsequently died from a blocked airway. The doctor argued that even if she had attended she would not have intubated the patient. The HL confirmed the **Bolam** test but held that if the medical opinion was not capable of withstanding logical analysis the judge would be entitled to hold it was not reasonable or responsible. On the facts of the case, although there was conflicting medical evidence, the HL held that her action was supported by a responsible body of medical opinion which was not illogical. Both **Bolam** and **Bolitho** were followed in **R v Royal National Orthopaedic Hospital NHS Trust 2012**, where the court held that in most cases the fact that distinguished experts in the field were of a particular opinion would demonstrate that the opinion was reasonable. However, the court also held that in rare cases, if the opinion was incapable of withstanding logical analysis judges were entitled not to use it to assess the standard of care expected.

A further point, made by the court in **Wilsher v Essex AHA**, is that although a junior doctor would be expected to show the standard of a qualified doctor (which accords with the principle in **Nettleship v Weston** that D is judged against a 'normal, competent person') the post the doctor is in will be relevant, so that the standard expected of a junior doctor will be less than that expected of a consultant.

Note that the 'balancing factors' are still relevant in cases where there is a subjective element such as age or professional competence. In **McDonnell v Holwerda 2005**, the question was whether a general practitioner (GP) had fallen below the standard expected of a reasonably competent GP by not recognising the possibility of meningitis in a child, following an examination. The court held that she had not fallen below the standard expected on the first occasion that she assessed the child. However, the GP had seen the child on a second occasion and, as the degree of risk was high due to the fact that the meningitis infection spreads so quickly, and the potential harm could be serious as meningitis can kill, the standard expected was higher. She had fallen below this standard because she had not carried out a full enough investigation, i.e., she had not taken reasonable precautions against the risk.

In **Ministry of Justice v Carter 2010**, the court was concerned with whether a GP in the prison service was negligent in not referring a prisoner for a specialist opinion after she reported feeling a lump in her breast. The GP had conducted a breast examination without detecting any abnormality so no referral was made. When C later developed cancer she sued the MOJ. The court found D negligent but on appeal it was made clear that in determining what should have been done by the doctor, the judge should have applied the principles from the cases of **Bolam v Friern HMC** and **Bolitho v City & Hackney HA**. On the evidence there was a responsible body of medical opinion that would have done the same as D and not have made a referral. As in my example above, there was no breach of duty and D's appeal was allowed.

There are plenty of other cases on breach. For more examples look back at the 'duty' cases. In **Vernon Knight Associates v Cornwall CC 2013** the council had not reached the standard expected of a reasonable council because there was a known risk of flooding and they had failed to take precautions against that risk by keeping the drains clear. They were therefor in breach of their duty to local residents.

Task 3

Remember that in order to even consider breach there must first be a duty, so any case you see where breach is an issue will be an example of someone owing someone else a duty even if no breach was proved. Look back at the facts of the following cases on breach of duty and state who owed a duty to whom. The first is done for you as an example.

> *Bolton v Stone – the cricket club owed a duty to passers-by*
>
> *Paris v Stepney BC*
>
> *Watt v Hertfordshire CC*
>
> *Latimer v AEC*
>
> *Nettleship v Weston*
>
> *Mullin v Richards*
>
> *Bolam v Friern HMC*
>
> *McDonnell v Holwerda*
>
> *Vowles v Evans*

Examination tip

It is clear from the cases that the standard expected will always depend on the particular circumstances. Look carefully at the facts of a scenario for clues e.g., mention of D's profession or age. Then apply the factors as appropriate, e.g., mention of something happening often indicates a high degree of risk, mention of a social activity indicates the risk may be justifiable. Balance the relevant factors as the court would do and conclude as to whether D is likely to be in breach of duty.

Task 4

Choose any 3 cases seen so far and consider which factors may have been relevant in deciding whether there was breach of a duty of care. See how many of them you can apply, as I did with **Bolton v Stone** above.

Summary

Breach is based on the standard of the reasonable person. The circumstances are relevant so D will be compared to a reasonable person in the same circumstances e.g.:

> *Reasonable parent*
>
> *Reasonable employer*
>
> *Reasonable child*
>
> *Reasonable doctor*

What is deemed reasonable is based on 4 factors:

> *The magnitude or degree of risk*
>
> *The gravity or seriousness of potential harm*
>
> *Whether the risk was justifiable*
>
> *The expense and practicality of taking precautions*

Task 5

Draw up the summary into a diagram, adding a case on each, and keep it for revision.

Self-test Questions on breach

In which case was the objective standard explained, and by whom?

What standard is expected of a professional?

What standard is expected of a child?

*Why had the employer not breached their duty in **Maguire v Harland & Wolff plc 2005?***

Causation

"... children's ingenuity in finding unexpected ways of doing mischief to themselves and others should never be underestimated" - Lord Hoffmann

The third matter that must be proved before D is liable is causation. C not only has to prove that damage occurred, but must also prove D's act or omission was the cause of that damage, both in fact and in law. Damage must be factually caused by D's breach and be reasonably foreseeable.

Causation in fact: the 'but for' test

The question here is whether D's breach in fact caused the damage. The courts apply the 'but for' test. This asks, "but for' D's negligence would the harm have occurred?" If the answer is "no" then D is liable. However, if the damage would have happened regardless of the negligent act or omission, D will not be liable for it.

Example

Using an earlier case, **Paris v Stepney BC**, we can see that 'but for' the employer's breach of duty (not making sure the employee wore goggles) the employee would not have been injured in the eye. The breach therefore factually caused the harm. Had the worker been injured in the arm then wearing goggles would not have prevented this. In that case we would say that 'but for' the breach the employee would still have been injured, so the breach did not factually cause the harm.

Key case

The leading case is **Barnett v Chelsea & Kensington HMC 1968**. A man suffering from vomiting and pain called at a hospital, but he was sent home without being treated. He later died of arsenic poisoning and his widow sued the hospital management committee. The hospital clearly owed a duty to patients, and was found to be in breach of this duty as the man was not even given an examination. However, they were not liable in negligence because he would have died regardless of whether he was treated. Here the answer to "But for D's negligence would the harm have occurred?" was "Yes, it would", so D was not liable. Both duty and breach were proved, but the claim failed on the 3rd issue, that of causation.

In **Bolitho v City & Hackney HA**, discussed with breach of duty, the doctor had argued that the patient would have died even if she had attended promptly. The HL confirmed that the **Bolam/Bolitho** test applied to causation as well as breach and that, as there was a logical body of medical opinion that would not have taken the particular action to save the patient (intubation of the airway), it could not be said that her lack of doing so caused his death. It is likely that, as in **Barnett v Chelsea & Kensington HMC**, he would have died anyway.

In **Dalling v R J Heale & Co 2011**, C had suffered injuries while drunk and claimed these were causally related to an earlier head injury which had impaired his ability to control his drinking. He had successfully sued D for the first incident but D now argued that the second injury was caused by C's voluntary drinking and not by the earlier injury. The court held that 'but for' the original head injury C would not have suffered the second injury because the first incident contributed to his lack of control, and also the harm was foreseeable and not too remote (see causation in law below). The evidence showed that C rarely drank to excess before the incident. D was liable.

Successive and multiple causes

In cases where there is more than one possible cause of harm a claim could fail if causation could not be proved in respect of any particular D. This is because if there is more than one breach, the 'but for' test can be hard to satisfy.

Example

Carl works for two employers both of whom have been negligent and exposed him to chemicals. He becomes sick and has to take several months off work. He wants to claim in negligence for the harm caused. The problem for Carl is that he cannot prove which exposure caused the sickness so cannot say but for one particular employer's negligence the disease would not have occurred.

This problem can occur where breaches follow after each other (successive causes) and where there is more than one breach and any one of them could have been the possible cause (multiple causes, as in my example), and in such cases the rules have been modified.

The court in **Performance Cars Ltd v Abraham 1962** held that in most cases of successive causes the original person in breach will be liable. Thus C could not claim from a later negligent driver for repairs to his car previously damaged in a similar accident by another driver. It was the original driver who had caused the damage (which had not yet been repaired).

Another case where there were successive causes is **Wright v Cambridge Medical Group 2011**. A GP was found liable in negligence for the late referral of a baby to hospital where, if she had received effective treatment in time, she would probably have made a full recovery. The doctor had argued that although negligent in the late referral this had not caused the harm (damage to her hip from an infection at the hospital) and that the harm was caused by the later negligent hospital treatment. The CA held that in cases of successive causes of harm, if it was foreseeable that harm could be caused by D's original breach of duty then it was right to hold D liable. It was foreseeable a late referral could cause harm and D's negligence significantly contributed to C's permanent injury. The same principle was applied in **Dalling v RJ Heale & Co** above. D was liable for C's head injury which caused him behavioural problems. Three years after the initial accident he fell over while drunk and injured himself. The evidence showed that he rarely drank before the first accident. The CA confirmed the judge's decision that D was liable for the later injury (although damages were reduced by a third for C's contributory negligence). The second injury was foreseeable because of his behavioural problems caused by the first negligent event.

Multiple causes are treated slightly differently and the rule from the case of **Fairchild** is used. In **Fairchild v Glenhaven Funeral Services Ltd 2002** the HL made clear that the 'but for' test is *necessary* but not always *conclusive*, and modified the rules.

Key case

The facts of **Fairchild** were that C became ill after exposure to asbestos dust in the course of successive employments. The CA had held that he could not recover damages from any of the employers, since he could not establish which period of employment had caused his illness. This seemed unfair to C, because each of the employers could be shown to be in breach of duty. It just wasn't clear which particular breach was the cause of the illness. The HL reversed the CA's decision and held that if C could show that D had 'materially increased the risk' of harm then the causation test could be satisfied. The HL said that the causation rules might be modified on policy grounds 'in special circumstances'.

In **Barker v Corus UK Ltd 2006**, with similar facts, the HL developed the rule in **Fairchild v Glenhaven Funeral Services Ltd** and held that the **Fairchild** exception to the 'but for' test could apply when there is more than one possible cause of harm, even if these include causes which would not usually lead to an action in tort (in this case a period of self-employment). Where there was more than one cause, damages would be apportioned according to how far each D had materially increased the risk of injury. So the **Fairchild** rule is that if there are several possible breaches anyone who had materially increased the risk of injury could be liable to pay damages for the whole of the amount of harm. **Barker** extends this to cases where some of the causes were not breaches (although, of course, only those in breach can be liable), but allows for the damages to be apportioned according to how much a particular D contributed to the risk of harm, rather than one D being liable in full. The next case extends the rule to where there is only one possible cause, although it does not affect the apportionment principle because if there is only one breach that cannot apply.

In **Costello v Grief 2011**, the Supreme Court looked again at a case involving mesothelioma allegedly caused by asbestos. Mrs Costello died and her estate claimed that the cause was exposure to asbestos during her employment in a factory. The trial judge held that causation had not been proven because she had not proved the risk had been doubled by her exposure, the evidence was that it had only increased her risk of harm by 18%. The CA held that, as per **Fairchild v Glenhaven Funeral Services Ltd**, it was only necessary to show the breach 'materially increased the risk' of harm. The Supreme Court agreed and held that **Fairchild** applied even in single exposure cases (where there was only one cause of harm and therefore only one D). Furthermore a risk was material if it was more than 'de minimis'. This means the word 'materially' is interpreted widely, and the breach need not be the main cause, or even a high percentage of it.

The idea of apportioning damages between different Ds as established in **Barker v Corus UK Ltd** was reversed by an amendment to the **Compensation Act 2006**, which provides in **s 3** that in mesothelioma cases each person who contributes to the harm is liable for the *whole* of the damages. However the Act only applies to mesothelioma cases so **Barker** will still be good law for other types of claim.

In **Milton Keynes Borough Council v Nulty 2013**, a fire had started in a recycling centre and one of the possible causes was a cigarette end dropped by someone working there. The CA said that in deciding whether something was the cause the court must ask itself whether the suggested explanation was more likely than not to be true. The judge had concluded that a cigarette end carelessly discarded by D was the most probable cause of the fire. There were other possibilities but these were unlikely. The evidence for believing that D had caused the fire was stronger than the evidence for not so believing. The CA upheld the decision. There may have been more than one *possible* cause, but, as there was only one *probable* cause, this sufficed to find D liable.

Multiple causes are often seen in medical cases. In **Bailey v Ministry of Defence and another 2008**, hospital negligence and an infection had led to a woman becoming weak. She later had other treatment elsewhere and suffered brain damage. The later treatment was not negligent so she sued the first hospital. The hospital argued it was not only their negligence that made her weak, but also the infection, and that a contribution to the risk of injury was not enough to prove causation. The judge disagreed, the correct question was whether the negligence had 'caused or materially contributed to' the injury, and it had. The CA upheld the decision and held that as long as D's act made a material contribution to the harm, causation could be proved, even if there was another, non-negligent, cause which also made a material contribution.

Fairchild v Glenhaven Funeral Services Ltd and **Barker v Corus UK Ltd** suggest that if there is a possibility that D's act caused the harm causation may be proved, even if it was not probable that it did so.

Despite the comment about 'special circumstances' in **Fairchild v Glenhaven Funeral Services Ltd**, the principle was extended to a different type of case in **Chester v Afshar 2004**. Here C had back problems and needed an operation. She was not told that there was a small risk of nerve damage. She had the operation and suffered such damage. The surgeon had breached his duty by not warning her, but had this caused the nerve damage? The answer to the question "But for the lack of warning would the harm have occurred?" may well have been "Yes," it might have happened anyway. However, the HL allowed her claim on the basis that although there was evidence that after taking further advice she *might* still have had the operation, she would have not had it *at that time*. The lack of warning had therefore caused the damage. This case again suggests that if there was a *possibility* that D's breach caused the harm, rather than a *probability*, causation may still be proved.

However, the next case shows that the exception to the 'but for' test is limited. In **Clough v First Choice Holidays 2006**, the CA confirmed that the rule in **Fairchild** had limited application. A holidaymaker had been injured when he slipped on a wall by a swimming pool and broke his neck. He argued that the travel company had breached the standard of care expected by not painting the wall with non-slip paint. He was drunk at the time but argued that the failure to use non-slip paint had materially increased his chance of falling (as per **Fairchild**). The judge ruled that causation was not proved. C had not shown that but for the breach of duty it was 'more likely than not' the accident would not have happened.

These are complicated rules so let's sum up.

The basic test comes from **Barnett v Chelsea & Kensington HMC** and provides that if the harm would not have occurred 'but for' D's breach factual causation is proved.

Fairchild v Glenhaven Funeral Services Ltd modifies the rule where there are several possible breaches, so that even if C cannot say 'but for' a particular D's breach the injury would not have occurred, causation will still be proved if any one D materially increased the risk of harm. Anyone who contributed in this way can be liable for the full damages.

Barker v Corus UK Ltd adds that where there are several possible causes, including non-negligent ones, damages can be apportioned between any Ds who materially contributed to the risk of harm.

The **Compensation Act** provides that C can claim the total damages from any one D who contributes to the risk of harm rather than apportion them between the Ds. However, this only applies in mesothelioma cases.

Costello provides that 'materially increased' can be anything more than 'de minimis' (here an 18% increase in risk). This case also shows that the **Fairchild** exception to the 'but for' test can apply even where there is only one possible D.

In **Fairchild v Glenhaven Funeral Services Ltd** the HL referred to the exception applying in 'special circumstances' and the exception to the 'but for' test was not applied in **Clough**.

Example

Hannah has an operation and due to Dr Walker's negligence and the fact that she develops a heavy cold she becomes quite weak. She transfers to another hospital where Dr Ross performs a second operation. Dr Ross has not been negligent but because Hannah is weak and had two operations close together she gets a lung infection. If the lung infection would have occurred regardless of the earlier negligence (e.g., if there is evidence it was solely due to the heavy cold) she will not be able to prove causation. If she can say "but for' the first hospital's negligence I would probably not have got the lung infection' she will be able to prove causation. The problem lies in the fact that it is not clear whether it was the negligence alone that caused her to get the infection. This is where the test needs to be modified according to **Fairchild**. If there is insufficient medical evidence to establish the 'but for' test it will be enough to show that the negligence materially increased the risk of harm. As Hannah was weak partly because of the negligence she should succeed in proving causation, as in **Bailey** above. Dr Walker will be liable for the full damages as per **Fairchild**. There is no other person in breach so damages cannot be apportioned as in **Barker**.

Loss of chance

The HL refused to extend this idea of 'possible' rather than 'probable' causes to allow compensation for *loss of chance* in **Gregg v Scott 2005**. Here a doctor negligently misdiagnosed C's cancer. If treated earlier the cancer might not have spread. It was shown that he had previously had a 45% chance of surviving 10 years. This had fallen to 25%. The judge held that even though there was a reduced chance, the chance of survival was still under 50%. The late diagnosis had not made sufficient difference to the result. On appeal the HL accepted that there *could* be a claim for a loss of chance 'when overall fairness so requires'. However, they held that a complete adoption of 'possible' rather than 'probable' causation was too great a change in the law and should be left to Parliament. C's appeal was rejected.

Collett v Smith & Another 2008 involved a successful claim for loss of chance. In 2003, at age 18, C injured his leg after a tackle, while playing for Manchester United reserve team. He was still given a two-year contract with the club, but as he never regained the same level of competence it was not renewed in 2005. He played for other clubs abroad but retired when he realised he would never have a successful career. He then commenced a claim for his lost chance of a football career. The court had to decide whether, 'but for' D's negligence, he would have succeeded in making a career in professional football and, if so at what level and for how long. There was evidence, most significantly from Sir Alex Ferguson, that he would have done well at the club, quite likely playing at Championship and

Premiership level. He won his claim and was awarded nearly four million pounds based on the lost chance of a successful career.

Even if D's act was found to be the factual cause of the harm, there is still one more hurdle for C to surmount. The harm must not be 'too remote' from D's breach of duty.

Causation in law: Remoteness of Damage

The test here is one of foreseeability. If the loss or damage is not foreseeable it is said to be 'too remote' from the breach. This was established in **The Wagon Mound 1961**, which replaced the wider test in **Re Polemis 1921**, that you were liable for *all* the direct consequences of your negligent actions.

Example

Your teacher negligently spills coffee over you and you have to change your clothes. This makes you late leaving college and by this time a storm has started. As you cycle home your bike is struck by lightning and you are injured. It can be said that 'but for' your teacher spilling coffee you would not have been delayed and so would not have been struck by lightning and injured. However the lightning is not foreseeable so is too remote from the breach. Causation in law is therefore not proved.

The full name of **The Wagon Mound** is **Overseas Tankship (UK) Ltd v Morts Dock & Engineering Co 1961**, but it is commonly called **The Wagon Mound.** The test from this case is that D is only liable for the foreseeable consequences of any breach of duty.

Key case

In **The Wagon Mound** oil was negligently spilt by the Ds. This oil caused a fire that damaged C's wharf two days later. The Ds were not liable because it was not believed that this type of oil could catch fire on water. The damage to the dock by *oil* was foreseeable, so C could claim for this, but not damage caused by the later *fire*. That damage was too 'remote' from D's act, because it was not foreseeable.

intervening act

Sometimes something happens between D's negligent act and C's injury. This is referred to by the Latin tag *'novus actus interveniens'* or in modern parlance, 'new act intervening'. Such an act may sometimes break the chain of causation between D's act or omission and the harm to C. In **Smith v Littlewoods 1987**, an owner of a disused cinema had left his property unsecured and vandals broke in. They caused a fire which spread to a neighbour's property. The neighbour sued the cinema owner. The claim failed. D successfully argued that the act of the vandals had broken the chain between the omission (not locking up properly) and the damage. An example of the argument failing can be seen in a case we looked at earlier, **Reeves v MPC**. The police argued that the prisoner's suicide was an intervening act, which broke the chain of causation. The HL did not accept this as it was foreseeable (the police knew he was a suicide risk).

In **Corr v IBC Vehicles Ltd 2008**, a widow had claimed damages in respect of her husband's suicide six years after he had an accident at work. The issue was whether the suicide was foreseeable, i.e., whether the breach had *caused* the suicide or whether it was too *remote*. The trial court found that the suicide was not foreseeable and that, based on **The Wagon**

Mound, foreseeability was an essential requirement of establishing both duty and damage caused. The CA reversed this decision and restated that as long as the type of harm was foreseeable the particular outcome need not be. The HL upheld the CA's decision. Several issues arose, but the main ones concerned causation, specifically foreseeability and breaking the chain. The HL held that severe depression was foreseeable and as it was of a similar type to depression there was no need for suicide itself to be foreseeable. The suicide did not break the chain of causation as it was not a conscious voluntary act, but a response to his depression.

Overlap

Note the overlap between foreseeability and intervening act. An intervening act will only break the chain of causation if it was unforeseeable itself.

Example

In **Reeves v MPC**, the prisoner was on suicide watch so suicide was foreseeable and didn't break the chain. If the police had left the door flap open and a mouse had crawled in through the hole and then bitten the prisoner who happened to suffer a rare allergy to mouse bites and died, this would be an unforeseeable event and so would be likely to break the chain between the negligence of the police and the death.

type of damage

If the *type* of damage is foreseeable, then the fact that it occurred in an unforeseeable way, or that the consequences were more extensive than could be foreseen, will not affect liability. In **Hughes v Lord Advocate 1963**, a child knocked over a paraffin lamp which caused an explosion. He was very badly burnt. The court found that the *type* of injury was foreseeable (burns) even though the way this had occurred (an explosion) was not. D was liable.

The principles of both **The Wagon Mound** and **Hughes** were confirmed by the HL in **Jolley v Sutton LBC 2000**.

Key case

In **Jolley,** a 14-year old boy was badly injured when working with a friend on an abandoned and derelict boat on council land. The CA had held that the council were not liable. Whilst it may be foreseeable that children might *play* on such a boat it was not foreseeable that they would attempt to *repair* it. The HL reversed the decision and made the point in the opening quote that the ingenuity of children should not be underestimated. It was foreseeable that they would meddle with the boat in some way – it did not matter that they had been repairing it rather than playing on it.

In **Hadlow v Peterborough CC 2011**, a teacher was working at a secure unit for young women who could be prone to violence. She should have had a member of the unit's care staff with her during lessons. When she noticed that the staff who escorted the three women to the lesson had both left and locked the door behind them, she jumped up to call out to them before they were out of earshot. In her hurry she tripped and injured herself. The issue to be decided was one of causation. It was accepted that had one of the women attacked her the unit would have been liable, as they were in breach of duty by not ensuring she had someone with her. However, the unit argued that their breach did not cause the harm because she had not been attacked – she injured herself by tripping over her chair. The CA, following **Hughes v Lord Advocate**, held that as the type of injury was foreseeable (the breach of duty had exposed the teacher to the risk of harm) even though it happened in an unforeseeable way (her attempt to remove the risk by getting the attention of the staff) the unit was liable.

Application/Food for thought

The **Hughes** test seems much wider than **The Wagon Mound**. It suggests that the harm itself does not necessarily have to be foreseeable. It would appear that the wider principle is correct because it was approved by the HL in **Jolley v Sutton LBC** and seen again in **Hadlow**.

Examination tip

It may be important to refer to **Jolley**, not just **The Wagon Mound** test, if the scenario involves children. Use **The Wagon Mound** as setting the test, but go on to mention the point made in **Jolley** that the ingenuity of children should not be underestimated. This could mean that something that would not be foreseeable where adults were concerned, and so would fail the test for legal causation under the **Wagon Mound**, would be foreseeable in the case of a child who can be expected to do the unexpected.

Task 6

Use two cases that you remember from looking at duty or breach. Use the 'but for' test to apply causation *in fact*. Then add the rules from **The Wagon Mound** and **Jolley v Sutton LBC** to see if D *legally* caused the harm.

the thin skull rule

There is another apparent exception to the foreseeability test. It is a common law rule that D must take the victim as he or she is found. This means that if a particular disability in the victim means they are likely to suffer more serious harm, or die, D is still liable, even though a person without that disability would not have been so seriously harmed. An example is **Smith v Leech Brain 1962**, where D's negligence caused a small burn, which activated a latent cancer from which C died. His wife sued his employer and the court held that C's particular vulnerability (the pre-existing cancer) did not affect liability. C's wife did not have to prove that cancer was foreseeable, only that some harm was, even though it was of a different type. It is called the 'thin' or 'egg shell' skull rule because the essence of the rule is that if there is something which makes V more vulnerable than other people this will not affect D's liability.

Example

Jake is riding his bike too fast and knocks over a man who has a very thin skull. Most people would have only suffered a few knocks and bruises, but this man dies because as he fell his skull broke open. Jake can be liable for the death, not just the foreseeable injuries, under the 'thin skull' rule.

Summary

When applying the law ask the following questions.

> *Would the harm have occurred 'but for' D's act or omission?*

Is there more than one cause? If so the test may be modified.

Was the harm foreseeable or was it too remote?

Was this type of harm foreseeable?

Does the thin-skull rule apply?

Task 7

Apply the law on duty, breach and causation to the facts of **Barnett v Kensington & Chelsea HMC**.

Self-test questions on causation

What is the 'but for' test and from which case did it come?

Which case established the rule on foreseeability?

*What did **Hughes** add to this?*

Can you explain the 'thin-skull rule'?

*What was the point made in **Jolley v Sutton LBC** (in the HL) in regard to children?*

"... liability can, and in my opinion should, be founded squarely on the principle established in Hedley Byrne itself" - Lord Goff

Where the loss is financial rather than physical, liability is more limited. This is based on policy and what is known as the 'floodgates' argument. In **Ultramares v Touche 1931**, Cardozo CJ said that allowing claims for pure economic loss would lead to liability *"in an indeterminate amount, for an indefinite time and to an indeterminate class"* i.e., it would open the 'floodgates' to claims. A distinction is made between economic loss and *pure* economic loss. A great many claims involve economic loss of some sort, e.g., loss of earnings would be a result of many physical injuries and is included in the claim for damages for that injury. However, where there is no physical damage, either to person or property, any such claim would usually fail because the loss is *only* (or 'purely') economic.

Example

You are walking to work when you see someone screaming that her husband has been hit by a car. You stop to help, though he is not badly hurt. As a result, you are late for a meeting, which means you lose an important contract. You also lose a day's pay. The husband can claim for his injuries and for loss of earnings whilst off work. The wife may have a claim for psychiatric harm, which will also include any loss of earnings. However, *your* loss of earnings was not a result of either physical or psychiatric harm so you cannot claim. In all three cases there is economic loss (earnings). Only in the last is it *pure* economic loss and so not recoverable.

The law also makes a distinction between economic loss caused by negligent statements (or, more correctly, misstatements), and economic loss caused by negligent acts. In this Chapter we will look at the rules for finding a duty in respect of negligent misstatements, and see that there is no duty in respect of negligent acts.

Negligent misstatements

The law has developed over the years and since 1963 the rule that no negligence claim involving pure economic loss could succeed has been eased in cases where the loss is a result of a negligent statement, rather than a negligent act.

Key case

The leading case is **Hedley Byrne v Heller 1963,** where the HL approved a dissenting judgment by Denning LJ in **Candler Crane v Christmas 1951.** Lord Denning had argued that accountants owed a duty not only to their employer, but also to anyone to whom they showed the accounts. This would include people that they knew their employer would show them to but not *"strangers of whom they have heard nothing and to whom their employer without their knowledge may choose to show the accounts"*. This was accepted and developed in **Hedley**. A bank gave a credit reference in which they negligently stated that their client was sound. The Cs relied on this and consequently suffered heavy losses when the client went into liquidation. On the facts the claim failed due to a disclaimer. However the *principle* was established that there could be liability in tort for such losses if there was a 'special relationship' between C and D.

The neighbour principle from **Donoghue v Stevenson**, used for cases of physical harm, was held to be too wide. Lord Reid said statements had to be treated differently for the following reasons:

words can spread further than acts

people in a social situation may make statements less carefully than they would in a business one

In cases involving statements therefore, there needs to be greater proximity between D and C, there must be a 'special relationship'.

The special relationship

Essentially a 'special relationship' means that:

D (the maker of the statement) possesses a special skill

C reasonably relies on D's statement

D knows that C is 'highly likely' to rely on the statement

There is an overlap between these three points. The more special someone's skill is, the more reasonable it is to rely on it. This is best illustrated by cases.

Examination tip

Cases are always important when dealing with a problem question, so make sure you know at least one for each part of proving a special relationship.

D possesses a special skill

Mutual Life and Citizen's Assurance Co v Evatt 1971 and **Esso Petroleum v Marden 1976**, illustrate the 'special skill' aspect well. In the first case the claim failed because D was in the insurance business and the negligent advice was in respect of investments. The majority (3-2) held that only if D was in the business of giving that type of advice would a duty arise. The minority thought a duty could arise when D knew the statement would be reasonably relied on, even if they were not in that particular line of business.

The minority view was applied in **Esso Petroleum v Marden.** Esso gave a negligent estimate of the potential turnover of a garage to the prospective buyer. This was not within their area of expertise, but the court held that they were liable. They knew that the statement would be relied on and they had implied that they had expertise so it was also reasonable for the Cs to rely on the statement.

Again, in **Lennon v MPC 2004**, a personnel officer gave negligent advice to a police officer about the effect of a break in employment on his housing benefit. Even though the personnel officer was not skilled in giving advice about housing benefit, it was reasonable for the police officer to rely on the advice given to him and he had lost his benefit by so doing. The CA held that there was sufficient special relationship between them so that it was fair, just and reasonable to impose a duty.

These cases show how 'skill', 'knowledge' and 'reasonable reliance' overlap.

knowledge

In **JEB Fasteners Ltd v Mark Bloom 1983**, auditors prepared company accounts knowing the company needed finance. They knew that anyone considering a takeover of the company would rely on the accounts. They were thus liable. Note that the court did not require that they should be able to identify a particular individual who would rely on them. It was enough that they knew *someone* would rely on them.

Key case

Remember **Caparo v Dickman plc v Dickman 1990**, which established the 3-part test for proving a duty? This was a 'negligent misstatement' case. Auditors negligently prepared a company's accounts. They were held not liable to a purchaser of shares who had relied on them. This case shows how the 'knowledge' requirement can significantly limit cases. Because the auditors prepared the accounts for the company, not potential investors, they could not know Caparo, as potential investors, would rely on them.

It is therefore important when looking at a scenario to identify who knows what about whom.

Examples

The following two cases illustrate the 'knowledge' point well, as the facts are similar but the decision in each was different.

In **Stone & Rolls Ltd v Moore Stephens 2009**, the HL followed **Caparo** and held that the auditors of a company had a duty to take reasonable care in auditing the accounts, but this duty was owed to the company in the interests of its shareholders, and did not extend to the company's creditors of whom they had no knowledge.

In **Law Society v KPMG Peat Marwick 2000**, a firm of accountants was hired to prepare annual reports for solicitors. This was a legal requirement and the reports would be passed by the solicitors to the Law Society, who administered a fund to compensate for any wrongdoing by lawyers. Due to the reports being negligently prepared the Law Society paid out substantial sums in compensation and sued the accountants. The CA held that a duty of care was owed. **Caparo** could be distinguished because the accountants knew the reports would be passed to the Law Society and that the Law Society would rely on them.

In **Smith v Bush 1989**, the HL held a surveyor owed a duty to house buyers even though he prepared the survey not for the buyers, but for the building society lending them money. He owed a duty to the 3rd party buyers because it was quite obvious that they would rely on his survey and the surveyor knew this, it was quite normal for buyers to rely on such surveys. There were *obiter dicta* in **Smith** which suggest a commercial buyer, however, might fail. It is normal practice in commercial deals to have your own survey done, so a surveyor for the lender would not 'know' the buyer would rely on the survey – they would expect them to have their own survey done. The court felt there would only be a duty if it was "highly likely" C would rely on the statement.

In **Scullion v Bank of Scotland plc 2011**, in a claim regarding a negligent valuation, the trial judge relied on **Smith v Bush** in finding that a valuer owed a duty of care to the purchaser of the property. The CA however, reversed the decision and declined to follow **Smith v Bush**. It could be distinguished because this was for a 'buy-to-let' property, rather than a domestic purchase, and thus was of a commercial nature. Most people who buy a property in order to let it do not rely only on valuations prepared by a valuer instructed by the lender, but obtain their own valuation, unlike the case of a private buyer as in **Smith**. On these facts no duty of care was owed.

N.B. In **Smith**, as in **Hedley Byrne v Heller**, there was a disclaimer but by this time further protection could be found in the **Unfair Contracts Terms Act 1977**. This Act prohibits unreasonable exclusions of liability so in **Smith** D could not rely on the disclaimer to avoid liability.

In **Spring v Guardian Assurance plc 1993** the HL held that an employer owed a duty to an employee in respect of a negligent reference, as they knew it would be relied on by a potential employer. In this case the advice was not given *to* C but was *about* C. This further extends the duty owed to 3rd parties.

Task 8

Compare **Caparo v Dickman** and **JEB Fasteners Ltd v Mark Bloom**. They aren't too different, so why was a duty found in one and not the other?

reasonable reliance

Lord Reid said in **Hedley Byrne v Heller** that there would be no duty of care for statements made on a social occasion. This seems fair. It would not be 'reasonable' to rely on a piece of information passed on in a drunken moment at the Christmas party! It isn't an absolute rule though. For example in **Chaudhry v Prabhakar 1989,** a friend who negligently gave advice on buying a car was held to owe a duty to C. He had knowledge of such matters and she had reasonably relied on that knowledge.

In **Caparo v Dickman** the purpose of the information was relevant. It is not likely to be found reasonable to rely on information intended for someone else for a different purpose. However, in **Ross v Caunters 1980** a solicitor was found liable to a 3rd party, the beneficiary under his client's will, when he acted negligently and this resulted in the beneficiary losing financially. This was a major extension of the law at the time, because it appeared to relate to negligent *acts* rather than *statements*. However the HL found a solicitor owed a duty to a 3rd party in **White v Jones 1995** (see below), based on an "assumption of responsibility" for his professional advice.

Examination tip

Look for clues in the scenario, such as 'the accountants had been told that ...', or 'knowing there was a declared bidder ...'. Statements like this should alert you to the fact that D knows C will rely on the statement.

Assumption of responsibility

The principle of 'assumption of responsibility' was rooted in **Hedley Byrne v Heller** but more emphasis was put on it during the nineties. In **Henderson v Merrett Syndicates 1995**, the HL held that syndicate managers could owe their members (underwriters of insurance policies) a duty in tort as well as contract. That duty was to exercise reasonable skill and care. Lord Goff made the remark in the opening quote and added that where someone assumed responsibility for professional services, this would be enough to impose a duty in respect of those services.

Key case

In **White v Jones 1995**, two daughters had been cut out of their father's will. Before he died he changed his mind and instructed his solicitor to amend his will. Despite a reminder this was never done and the daughters did not receive their inheritance. The HL found the solicitors liable to the daughters for their losses. The emphasis was on the fact that the solicitor, as a professional, had 'assumed responsibility' for his work and thus was under a duty not to do it negligently. It is reasonable for beneficiaries of wills to rely on solicitors doing their jobs properly.

The majority based their decision on achieving "practical justice" and appear to be filling in a gap in the law in order to allow a 3rd party beneficiary (who has no contract with the solicitor and so cannot sue in contract law) to claim for the loss of their inheritance. (This is a good example of judicial creativity so can be related to Concepts of Law - AQA, or the Special Study Unit - OCR.)

The idea of 'assumption of responsibility' is related to the 'fair, just and reasonable' requirement from **Caparo v Dickman**. In **Phelps v Hillingdon BC 2001**, the CA held that an educational psychologist had not assumed responsibility for C when he failed to diagnose her dyslexia in a report made for the education authority. It was therefore not 'fair, just and reasonable' to impose a duty. The HL reversed this decision on the basis that a professional asked to work with a specific child could be liable to her for his lack of care and skill in the exercise of that profession. Similarly in **Carty v Croydon LBC 2005**, C sued the council for damages for failing to assess his special educational needs properly and failing to provide him with a suitable education. The CA held that an education officer was a professional and so there could be a duty if he had 'assumed responsibility' towards a child. Dyson LJ said that this would be based on the normal **Caparo** 3-part test of foreseeability, proximity and whether it was fair, just and reasonable to impose a duty.

The **Caparo** test was used again in the next case, this time without the assumption of responsibility angle.

In **Jain v Trent Strategic Health Authority 2009**, the Authority, concerned about both structural and health issues, closed a nursing home without prior notice. The proprietors successfully appealed against this but suffered economic loss to the business. At trial the judge held a duty of care was owed. The CA reversed the decision and allowed the appeal by the Health Authority, who successfully argued that the judge had erred in law in holding that it was fair, just and reasonable that it should owe a duty of care to the proprietors as it was well established that duties should only be held to exist either within existing categories or on an incremental basis, and that no similar duty had been found to exist. The CA approved **Caparo v Dickman,** and held it was not fair, just and reasonable to impose a duty of care when the Authority's primary duty was to the residents of the nursing home and to the public interest. The urgency of the situation and risk of harm to residents outweighed the economic interests of the proprietors. The HL confirmed the decision of the CA and held that although the Health Authority owed a duty to the residents of a nursing home this duty did not extend to the proprietors.

So it is clear that the **Caparo** test is still important in cases involving economic loss. However, the other tests may also need to be considered and the matter was summed up in the following case, which shows that no one test is absolute.

Key case

In **Customs and Excise Commissioners v Barclays Bank 2006**, the HL approved the tests for establishing a duty in cases of economic loss, which had been put forward by the CA. A bank had allowed money to be transferred out of two accounts, which had been frozen by Customs and Excise. This meant that the money owed to Customs by the companies involved could not be paid in full, so the Customs and Excise Commissioners sued the bank for the balance. The trial judge had found that the bank did not owe a duty to the 3rd party (Customs and Excise), mainly based on the lack of any 'assumption of responsibility'. In the CA, Longmore LJ had summarised the position. He said that the modern law derived from 4 cases, **Caparo v Dickman, Henderson v Merrett Syndicates, White v Jones** and **Phelps v Hillingdon BC**. In cases of economic loss it was appropriate to consider each of the following tests:

> the 3-fold Caparo test (foreseeability, proximity and whether it is fair, just and reasonable to impose a duty)

> the 'assumption of responsibility' test (White v Jones)

> the 'incremental' test (liability is not extended in a giant leap but in short steps)

He said that the tests merged into each other, and that although an 'assumption of responsibility' may sometimes be enough for a duty to exist, it was not always a *necessary* ingredient. The CA found that the bank owed a duty to Customs and Excise. The HL reversed the decision of the CA, but confirmed the tests. Lord Bingham said an assumption of responsibility was *"a sufficient but not a necessary condition of liability"*. If this test is satisfied, it may mean nothing further is needed, but if not then the other tests may need to be considered. Lord Mance said:

> *"The conceptual basis on which courts decide whether a duty of care exists in particular circumstances has been repeatedly examined. Three broad approaches have been suggested, involving consideration (a) whether there has been an assumption of responsibility, (b) whether a three-fold test of foreseeability, proximity and "fairness,*

justice and reasonableness" has been satisfied or (c) whether the alleged duty would be "incremental" to previous cases. ....All three approaches may often (though not inevitably) lead to the same result. Assumption of responsibility is on any view a core area of liability for economic loss."

On the facts the HL held that the bank had not assumed any responsibility towards the Commissioners. Nor was it fair, just and reasonable to impose a duty on the bank as it was not a party to the transaction between Customs and its creditors. Imposing a duty would not be analogous with or incremental to any previous development of the law. None of the tests was satisfied.

In **Calvert v William Hill Credit Ltd 2008**, a gambler argued the bookmaker owed him a duty of care and had breached it by letting him continue betting after he asked them to stop taking his money. This had caused him both financial ruin and psychological harm. The High Court found William Hill owed him a duty to take reasonable care to exclude him after his request. Applying the 3-stage test, there was sufficient proximity between the parties, harm was foreseeable because gambling is a recognised psychiatric disorder, and there was no policy reason such as the floodgates issue to exclude such a duty. The court also accepted his argument that William Hill had voluntarily assumed responsibility by acknowledging his request for help as a problem gambler and undertaking to exclude him. This follows **Customs and Excise Commissioners v Barclays Bank 2006**, where the HL said the tests were to be looked at together, not in isolation.

Task 9

Apply the rules on special relationship to the facts of **Smith v Bush**, then consider whether there was an assumption of responsibility in that case.

Summary of negligent misstatement

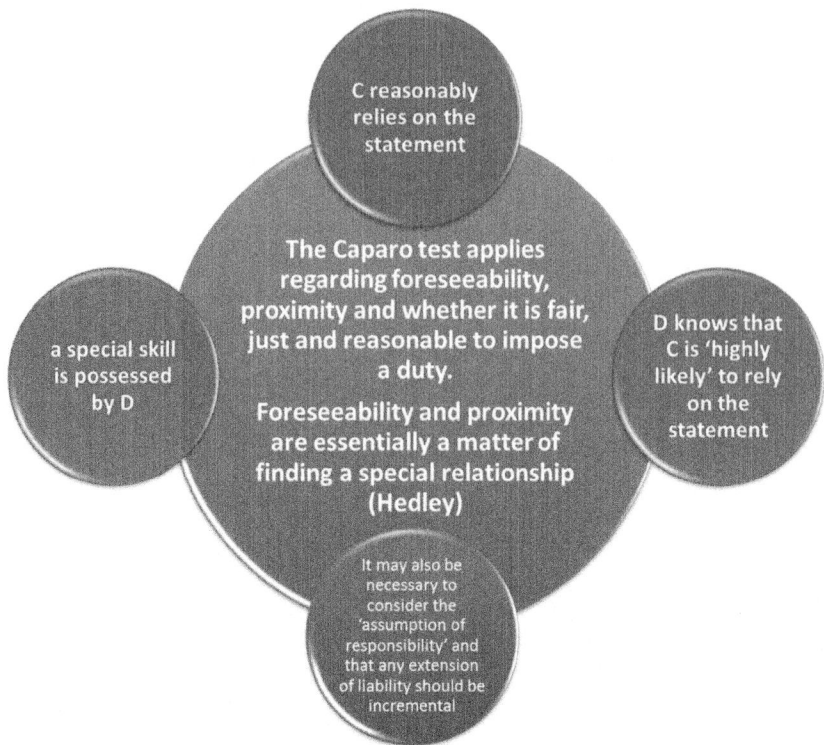

C reasonably relies on the statement

The Caparo test applies regarding foreseeability, proximity and whether it is fair, just and reasonable to impose a duty.

Foreseeability and proximity are essentially a matter of finding a special relationship (Hedley)

a special skill is possessed by D

D knows that C is 'highly likely' to rely on the statement

It may also be necessary to consider the 'assumption of responsibility' and that any extension of liability should be incremental

Examination tip

The law itself is not fully clear on which test to use so this can be difficult for candidates. **Customs and Excise Commissioners v Barclays Bank** can be used to explain that where there is an assumption of responsibility nothing else is usually needed, but in most other cases the **Caparo** test would need to be satisfied. Remember also that foreseeability, proximity and whether it is fair, just and reasonable to impose a duty will depend on satisfying the special relationship requirements from **Hedley Byrne v Heller**.

Economic Loss by acts

The question of whether economic loss could be claimed in respect of negligent acts was answered in the negative in **Spartan Steel and Alloys Ltd v Martin & Co 1973** by the CA.

Key case

In **Spartan Steel**, the Ds negligently severed a power cable to C's factory and caused damage to steel in production. The Cs were able to claim for the physical damage to the steel and for the consequential loss of profit on that steel, but not for further loss of profit due to other, undamaged, machines lying idle. This last sum was pure economic loss because it did not stem from any physical damage.

There is a case where a claim for pure economic loss has been successful, but this was where there was an exceptionally close proximity between C and D. In **Junior Books v Veitchi 1983**, a subcontractor was held liable to the owner of the premises he was working in and who had ordered the work (through the main contractor). This was almost a contractual relationship and so it sets no precedent for cases where the degree of proximity is less than this.

The rule against recovery for economic loss was reinforced by the HL in **Murphy v Brentwood DC 1990**. The Council's building inspector approved plans which meant C's property was poorly constructed and in a dangerous state. This led to a drop in its value. Reversing the decision of the CA, the HL held there was no duty. The judges appeared to have differing reasons for their decision but the result is that if there is a defect but it has not yet caused any damage, there is no duty. Of course, if the defect actually leads to damage the usual rules for physical harm would apply.

Example

A property is built according to a set of plans that were negligently prepared. The balcony is unstable, thus making the property worth less than it should be. This is a defect but there is no damage yet. The owners cannot claim as their loss is purely economic – i.e., a lower value. However if the balcony falls off then the house is now physically damaged and a claim can be made – make sense?

Examination tip

Note that proving a duty is just the first step in any negligence case. In order to win, C will still have to prove that the duty was breached, *and* that the breach caused the loss suffered. This may well be straightforward and if so do not spend too long on it, however both must always be mentioned as without them there cannot be liability.

Summary of cases on misstatements

Hedley Byrne v Heller 1963 – to establish sufficient proximity there has to be a 'special relationship' between D and C. This means:

D has a special skill

C reasonably relies on D's statement

D knows that C is 'highly likely' to rely on the statement

Mutual Life and Citizen's Assurance Co v Evatt 1971 – the Privy Council held that only if the defendants were in the business of giving that *type* of advice would a duty arise. The minority thought a duty could arise when D *knew the statement would be reasonably relied on.*

Esso Petroleum v Marden 1976 – Esso gave a negligent estimate of the potential turnover of a garage. This was not within their area of expertise but the court held that Esso was liable as they *knew* the statement would be relied on. It was also *reasonable to rely* on it.

Caparo v Dickman 1990 – the auditors prepared the accounts for the company, not potential investors so they could not *know* Caparo would rely on them. Thus it was not 'fair, just and reasonable' to impose a duty.

Smith v Bush 1989 – a surveyor owed a duty to a house buyer even if he prepared the survey for the building society, as he knew that the buyer would rely on his survey.

Chaudhry v Prabhakar 1989 – a friend who negligently gave advice on buying a car owed a duty to C as he had knowledge of such matters, so it was *reasonable* for her to rely on it.

Spring v Guardian Assurance plc 1993 – an employer owed a duty to an employee in respect of a negligent reference as they *knew* it would be relied on.

White v Jones 1995 – a solicitor, as a professional, had *'assumed responsibility'* for his work and thus was under a duty not to do it negligently.

Phelps v Hillingdon BC 2001 – a professional asked to work with a specific child could be liable to her for his lack of care and skill in the exercise of that profession.

Summary of cases on acts

Spartan Steel and Alloys Ltd v Martin & Co 1973 – C could claim for the physical damage to the steel and for the consequential loss of profit on that steel but not for further loss of profit due to other, undamaged, machines lying idle, which was pure economic loss.

Murphy v Brentwood DC 1990 – if no damage has yet been done, C cannot claim for the fact that the property is worth less than it should be because there is an inherent defect due to negligent building inspections.

Self-test questions on economic loss

What constitutes a special relationship?

*Why did the claim fail in the **Mutual Life** case?*

***Smith v Bush** shows a surveyor for a building society can owe a duty to a buyer. When might there not be such a duty?*

*On what was the emphasis in **White v Jones**?*

*How did Longmore LJ summarise the position in **Customs and Excise Commissioners v Barclays Bank?***

"In cases involving nervous shock, it is essential to distinguish between the primary victim and secondary victims. In claims by secondary victims the law insists on certain control mechanisms, in order, as a matter of policy, to limit the number of potential claimants" - Lord Lloyd

What is meant by psychiatric harm?

Also called 'nervous shock', psychiatric harm occurs when someone has suffered harm due to another's negligence, but that harm is psychiatric rather than physical. Psychiatric harm includes such things as post-traumatic stress, clinical depression and personality change. A claim in negligence for psychiatric harm requires the usual proof of duty, breach and causation. It is only the rules on duty that differ, depending on the type of harm. The courts tend to limit liability in such cases, mainly because of what is called the 'floodgates' argument. This means that because the number of potential Cs could be vast it could open the 'floodgates' to claims. The opening quote relates to this, it is from **Page v Smith,** discussed below.

Example

A drunk driver ploughs into a queue of people at a bus stop outside an office block. Many are killed or injured. Any of these people can claim in the normal way. The driver will owe them a duty based on foreseeability, proximity, and whether it is fair, just and reasonable to impose a duty (**Caparo v Dickman**). However, hundreds of other people may have seen the accident from the offices. If any of these people suffer psychiatric harm as a result of seeing the incident the rules on whether they are owed a duty of care by the driver will be stricter.

Examination tip

For problem questions the current law and a few example cases will be needed. The cases you select will depend on the scenario you are given. Essay questions on this area require knowledge of how the law has developed (although if you are studying for AQA there are no evaluation questions so you won't need this). The diagrams at the end of the Chapter will provide a revision guide on what you could include in each type of question.

For all students however, the current law will be better understood in the light of its development up to the case of **McLoughlin v O'Brien**, where a test for establishing a duty in cases of psychiatric harm was first provided by the HL. We'll therefore look at the development briefly before going on to the current rules.

Development

The first successful claim for nervous shock was **Dulieu v White 1901**. Here a person suffered shock when a van and horses drove into the pub where she was working (yes, horses – but note the date). It was held that the driver owed her a duty of care. The principle was established that in order to succeed C must be in fear for his or her own safety.

In **Hambrook v Stokes 1925**, a mother was successful in her claim when she suffered shock after seeing a runaway lorry careering towards her children. Although they were not harmed and she was not in danger herself the court recognised that the particularly close relationship between mother and child could bring her within the class of people to whom a duty was owed. She had also seen the incident herself. The principle here is that even if you are not in danger yourself, a particularly close relationship to someone who is may be enough *if* you see the incident with your own eyes.

In **Bourhill v Young 1943** a pregnant woman heard a crash and was so traumatised that she later gave birth to a stillborn baby. The court rejected her claim against the driver because she was some distance away and safe herself. No duty is owed where C is not in proximity to any foreseeable danger, as here.

In **King v Phillips 1952**, a mother suffered shock when she (wrongly) believed that her son had been run over by a taxi. She failed in her claim against the driver. The court held that injury *by shock* had to be foreseeable.

In **McLoughlin v O'Brien 1982**, the first case to reach the HL since **Bourhill v Young,** a test for dealing with cases of psychiatric harm was established.

The test from McLoughlin

Mrs McLoughlin was told about an accident in which her husband and children had been seriously injured; one child had, in fact, died. She went straight to the hospital where she saw them before they had been attended to. She suffered 'nervous shock' as a result. She sued the person who negligently caused the accident. In allowing her claim the HL held that there were three matters to consider in claims for nervous shock:

> *the relationship between C and the victim (usually parent and child or husband and wife)*

> *the proximity of C to the accident (in time and space)*

> *the means by which the shock was caused*

The HL confirmed and slightly expanded the test in the next case.

Key case

In **Alcock v CC of South Yorkshire 1991**, many people had been injured or killed in the Hillsborough football stadium disaster, these people suffered physical harm so could claim under the normal rules (**Caparo v Dickman**). There were also many claims from people who had been at the ground or had watched the news on television and knew that their loved ones were at the stadium. The HL confirmed that the **McLoughlin v O'Brien** test applied to these people, but said the relationship part of the test extended to those with 'close ties of love and affection'. There must also be a *sudden shock* and the shock must cause a *recognisable psychiatric illness* (mere grief is not enough). It was also said that those watching the events on television could not succeed. There were, however, *obiter dicta* to the effect that a live broadcast may be different. A hypothetical example was given of seeing live television pictures of a hot-air balloon catching fire knowing that your children were in it.

Task 10

Write a brief comparison of **Hambrook v Stokes** and **King v Phillips** to show why one succeeded and the other didn't.

The requirements for proving a duty of care as established in **McLoughlin v O'Brien** were referred to as 'control mechanisms' in **Alcock v CC of South Yorkshire**. This is because they control the number of people who can claim. However, before looking at *how* they apply, we need to consider to *whom* they apply. An important distinction was made in **Page v Smith 1995** between primary and secondary victims.

Primary and secondary victims

Key case

In **Page v Smith**, C was a passenger involved in a car accident and, although he was not physically hurt, his ME condition, which had been in remission, recurred. The HL drew a distinction between primary and secondary victims. A primary victim is someone who is directly affected and in danger of harm. A secondary victim is not directly affected, but a passive witness to the events. In all cases, *some* harm must be foreseeable, whether physical or psychiatric. However, in the case of secondary victims, only foreseeability of *psychiatric* harm, in a *'person of normal fortitude'*, will suffice. The HL held that here the C was a primary victim, so there was no need to prove that psychiatric harm was foreseeable. In the opening quote Lord Lloyd refers to secondary victims, he then goes on to say that the control mechanisms have no place where the C is a primary victim.

This case is also an example of the 'thin skull rule' – that you must take your victim as you find them. Under the thin-skull rule some harm must be foreseeable, but if it is then the fact that the C suffered greater harm due to a pre-existing weakness will not cause the claim to fail.

Task 11

Compare this case to the next one. Can you identify the difference between the passenger in **Page** and the police in **White**?

In a further case involving the Hillsborough disaster, **White v CC of South Yorkshire 1999**, police assisting at the scene claimed compensation for suffering psychiatric harm at seeing the horror of the event. The HL clarified the position on rescuers and restated the test for all secondary victims.

Key case

In **White**, the CA had suggested that as the police were rescuers there was no need to prove close ties to the victims. The HL reversed the decision, and held that rescuers could only succeed if their own safety were at risk. Lord Hoffmann restated the control mechanisms for secondary victims:

> *C must have close ties of love and affection with the victim. Such ties may be presumed in some cases (e.g., spouses, parent and child) but must otherwise be established by evidence*
>
> *C must have been present at the accident or its immediate aftermath*
>
> *The psychiatric harm must have been caused by direct perception of the accident or its immediate aftermath, and not upon hearing about it from someone else*

In **Donachie v Chief Constable of Greater Manchester 2004**, the issue of primary and secondary victims arose again. A policeman was instructed to attach a tag to the car of suspected criminals. It was parked near a pub where the suspects were drinking. His colleagues kept watch from the tracker van in case the suspects left the pub. He attached the device but it did not work. He made several trips to retrieve and then reattach it until it finally gave a signal. He became increasingly frightened of being caught by the suspects. Unknown to his employers, he had hypertension and suffered psychiatric harm that led to a stroke. The judge found they had been negligent as there was a history of problems with the tagging devices. The issue was which type of victim C was. The judge classed him as a secondary victim. He therefore had to prove *psychiatric* harm was foreseeable. As his employers did not know of his existing condition the harm was not foreseeable and they were not liable. On appeal C argued that he was a primary victim because there was a danger of being assaulted by the suspects. The CA agreed he had been in danger of harm and so a primary victim, and allowed his appeal.

In **Monk v Harrington 2008**, C had supervised the construction of a platform that collapsed, causing one death and several injuries. He went to the scene and offered assistance as a first-aider. He then suffered psychiatric harm and claimed damages from the employers of the crane driver, whose actions had actually caused the platform to fall. He said he was a rescuer and a primary victim because he believed he was in danger himself. He also argued that he believed he had been partly to blame for the accident and so was effectively a participant. The court agreed that he was a rescuer, but held he was not in danger himself and that any belief he had as to the danger he might be in had to be reasonable. On the evidence his belief that he was in danger was not reasonable. He was therefore a secondary victim and so subject to the **Alcock v CC of South Yorkshire** rules.

Although the primary/secondary distinction was specifically made in **Page v Smith**, examples of it can be identified in earlier cases, in particular those involving rescue situations. A comparison of the following cases will help show how the distinction applies in practice.

Rescuers

In **Chadwick v BTC 1967**, a rescuer at a train crash was successful in a claim for nervous shock after assisting at the scene for several hours. He can be regarded as a 'primary' victim because he was in danger at the time. If we compare this case to **McFarlane v Caledonia Ltd 1993** we can see how the primary/secondary distinction applies. In the latter case, a person on a support ship which rescued people from a fire on an oil rig was classed as a 'bystander' not a 'rescuer', because he was not in danger. He was not a primary victim so had to satisfy the test for secondary victims. As the ship had not got into close proximity to the disaster, and he had no close relationship with the victims, his claim failed. The court also repeated the point that C must be compared to a "person of ordinary fortitude and phlegm".

In **Greatorex v Greatorex 2000**, the slightly unusual question that arose was whether D owed a duty to a rescuer who was also his father. D was injured in a road accident as a result of his own negligence. His father was a fireman who assisted in the rescue and as a result suffered nervous shock. He brought an action against his son. It was held that D did not owe his father a duty of care for policy reasons. It would be *"undesirable and detrimental to family life and relationships"* for members of a family to sue each other. It was made clear that, following **White v CC of South Yorkshire,** where there is no personal risk, a rescuer is classed as a secondary victim and so has to satisfy the **McLoughlin v O'Brien/ Alcock v CC of South Yorkshire** control mechanisms.

Examination tip

The **McLoughlin/Alcock** control mechanisms confirmed in **White v CC of South Yorkshire** will be needed for a problem question. Reference to the primary/secondary distinction in **Page** will also be needed. Watch carefully for the type of harm suffered and whether C is in any danger. For primary victims the usual rules **(Caparo v Dickman)** apply. For secondary victims apply the mechanisms **(Alcock)**. You may also need to refer to the role of rescuers.

Task 12

Before reading on, look at the cases again and consider how the control mechanisms have been applied. See if you can spot any inconsistencies or difficulties yourself. Jot down your thoughts and keep this for essay questions.

The control mechanisms

Let's look at the control mechanisms in more detail to see how they apply.

Close ties of love and affection

In cases of physical harm there must be proximity between C and D. This means there must be some kind of legal relationship between them (e.g. manufacturer and consumer). In cases of psychiatric harm there must be proximity between C and the *victim*, and in this case the relationship is a personal one. It means C must have 'close ties of love and affection' with the victim. Such ties may be presumed in the case of spouses, or parent and child **(McLoughlin v O'Brien)** but must otherwise be established by evidence **(Alcock v CC of South Yorkshire).**

Example

Using my example from the beginning of the last chapter we can see that the woman would be able to satisfy this part of the test because a close relationship is presumed in the case of a spouse, and her husband is the victim. However you would not satisfy it because you are not in any danger, so if you suffered psychiatric harm due to the event you would have to prove close ties to the victim. As you have no relationship you will fail. (It is also unlikely you had a 'sudden shock' as the man was not badly hurt, so you would fail on this point too).

As regards rescuers, remember that if in danger themselves they would be primary victims and so the normal **Caparo** rules on duty would apply. If not they will be secondary victims and have to prove 'close ties' to the victim.

Immediate aftermath

This is also a question of proximity, but this time one of space and time. This means C must have proximity to the event (space – C witnesses the event or is nearby) or its 'immediate aftermath' (time - C must have been present at the time or shortly thereafter). A few examples will help explain this, although the cases have not always been entirely consistent. In **McLoughlin v O'Brien**, the mother heard about the accident an hour or so after it happened and went straight to the hospital, she was not at the scene but saw the immediate aftermath shortly afterwards at the hospital. In **Alcock v CC of South Yorkshire,** a lapse of 8 or 9 hours before going to the mortuary caused several claims to fail. In **Taylorson v Shieldness 1994**, the parents of a child who was seriously injured in an accident did not get to the hospital in time to see him properly before he was operated on. They stayed with him during the next 2 days until he died. The CA refused to extend the 'immediate aftermath' of the accident to the death two days later. In **Atkinson v Seghal 2003**, a mother arrived at the scene of a road accident to be told her daughter had been killed. The body had already been removed and she went to the mortuary. She then suffered a psychiatric illness. The trial court held that the visit to the mortuary was not within the immediate aftermath. The CA reversed this decision and held that the aftermath extended to the mortuary visit.

In **Taylor v A Novo (UK) Ltd 2013**, C suffered psychiatric harm after witnessing the sudden collapse and death of her mother who had been injured at work by D's negligence a few weeks earlier. The CA held that she was a secondary victim and referred to the 'control mechanisms' from **Alcock v CC of South Yorkshire**. In the case of secondary victims psychiatric injury must be a reasonably foreseeable consequence of D's negligence. Also, there must be a relationship of proximity between C and the victim. There was clearly a relationship of proximity between her and her mother, and if she had been in physical proximity to her mother at the time of the original injury she would have satisfied the tests. However, the event which caused the harm (her mother's death) was some weeks after the original negligence so the harm was not a foreseeable consequence of D's negligence. Cases such as **Atkinson v Seghal** could be distinguished. Her claim failed. This case shows that although there is not a clear cut-off point, the immediate aftermath cannot be extended indefinitely.

Examination tip

As you can see, the cases are not fully consistent so it is a good idea to use more than one to support your answer in respect of this part of the test. If there has been a gap between the event and the psychiatric harm you could use **Taylor v A Novo (UK) Ltd** to suggest the claim might fail, but if the time lapse is short you could use **McLoughlin v O'Brien** or **Atkinson v Seghal** to suggest it will succeed.

How the shock was caused

The means by which the shock was caused has generally been restricted to first-hand knowledge and would not include being told by a third party, nor to seeing events on television (**Alcock v CC of South Yorkshire**). In **Atkinson v Seghal**, the trial court had held that the shock was caused by the news of the death, not the visit to the mortuary, and so rejected her claim. The CA held that the illness was caused in part by the visit to the mortuary and not only by being told of the death by the police at the scene (which would be via a third party and so would not have been enough). Her appeal was allowed.

Anything else?

The HL in **Alcock v CC of South Yorkshire** also made clear that there must be a *sudden shock* and that the shock must cause a *recognisable psychiatric illness*. Medical evidence will be needed. The HL also said that *mere grief is not enough*.

In **Sion v Hampstead AHA 1994**, a father suffered psychiatric harm after watching his son deteriorate and die over a period of two weeks. Although the hospital had been negligent there was no liability to the father for the psychiatric harm because it was not caused by a sudden shock.

In **North Glamorgan NHST v Walters 2003**, a mother suffered psychiatric illness after sitting with her 10-month old baby as his condition deteriorated following the (admitted) negligence of the hospital. After 36 hours, his life support system was turned off. There were various reasons behind the CA's decision, but one issue was whether the 'sudden shock' requirement in **Alcock v CC of South Yorkshire** had been satisfied. The CA decided it was and allowed her claim for psychiatric harm caused by the hospital's negligence. This case is useful to compare to **Sion** to indicate that although a sudden shock is required, the courts treat this quite flexibly and also that while two weeks may be outside what can be termed 'sudden', two days may not be.

In **Vernon v Bosley 1997**, compensation was awarded to a father who saw his daughters' bodies retrieved from a car which had gone into the river. The court held that the 'abnormal' grief he suffered from seeing the immediate aftermath of the accident could not be distinguished from the 'normal grief' to be expected. He could therefore claim for both. This indicates that although 'mere grief' is not enough alone, as long as there is also an abnormal grief present then the test is satisfied.

Examination tip

Remember that proving a duty is just the first step in any negligence case. In order to win, C will still have to prove that the duty was breached, *and* that the breach caused the loss suffered. This applies whatever the type of harm and not recognising this is a common failing by candidates in examinations. You may not need to deal with these in any detail if the situation is clear but at least mention them briefly. Also if C is a primary victim you only need to discuss duty as per **Caparo v Dickman** and not go into the control mechanisms.

Example

In **Brown v Richmond upon Thames LBC 2012**, C suffered a mental breakdown caused by stress at work. The council knew he had work-related problems and had drawn up an action plan some time before. They were at fault in failing to implement this plan. As decided in **Page v Smith**, a primary victim is someone who is directly affected and in danger of harm, this was the case here so the normal rules applied.

Duty: The risk of harm was foreseeable as the council knew he had problems. Proximity was satisfied because there is a clear relationship between an employer and employee and it is not a novel situation. On the facts there was no policy reason to exclude liability and the claim would not open the floodgates to others. It was therefore fair, just and reasonable to impose a duty.

Breach: The duty was breached by the council's failure to implement the plan, which a reasonable employer would have done, taking into account that the risk of harm was known and it would have been relatively easy to put the plan in action i.e., take precautions.

Causation: Factual causation is proved because the psychiatric harm would not have occurred 'but for' their failure. Also, there is legal causation because the harm was foreseeable so it was not too remote from the breach of duty.

Summary of the developing principles

The first successful claim for nervous shock was in **Dulieu v White 1901** where it was held that C must be in fear for his/her own safety to succeed. The following is a summary of how law has developed over the years since then.

no duty is owed unless C is in foreseeable danger and in proximity to the accident	**Bourhill v Young 1943**
established the 3 matters to consider in nervous shock claims	**McLoughlin v O'Brien 1982**
confirmed the McLoughlin test but added 'close ties of love & affection' and that there must be a 'sudden shock' which caused a recognisable psychiatric illness	**Alcock v CC of South Yorkshire 1991**
distinction between primary and secondary victims drawn	**Page v Smith 1995**
reconfirmed the test but said that rescuers had to meet the test for secondary victims unless in danger themselves	**White v CC of South Yorkshire 1999**
Made clear the immediate aftermath could not be extended indefinitely	**Taylor v A Novo (UK) Ltd 2013**

For problem questions you need to follow a logical structure. Here is a brief summary.

Summary of the application of the rules

Has C suffered a recognisable psychiatric illness?

Is C a primary victim? Page vs. Smith

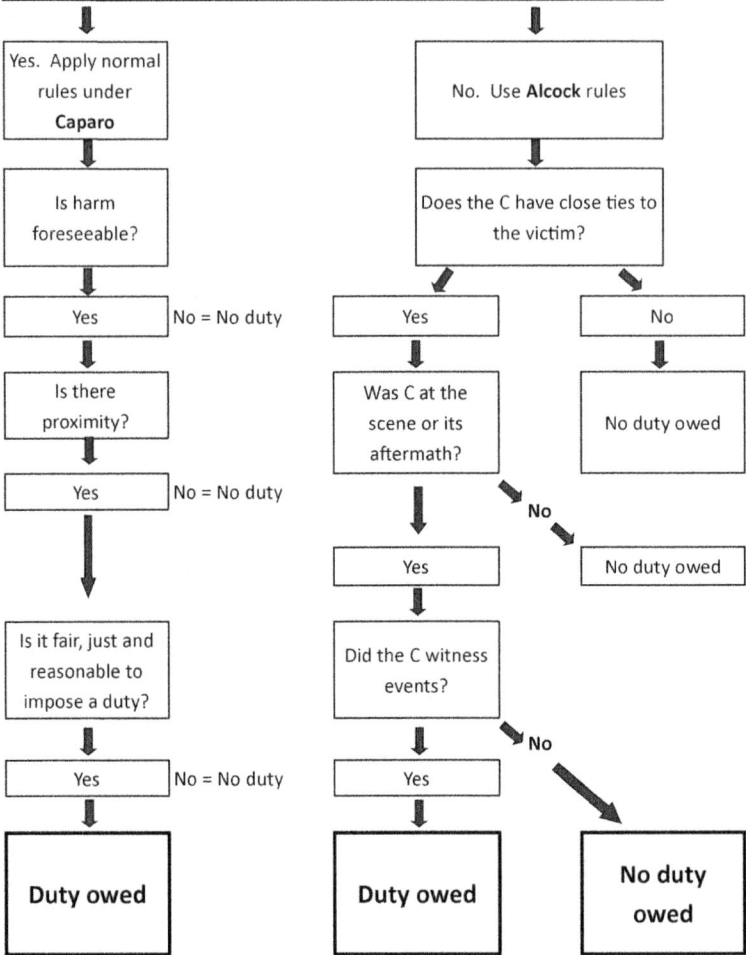

Left branch:

Yes. Apply normal rules under **Caparo**

↓

Is harm foreseeable?

↓

Yes | No = No duty

↓

Is there proximity?

↓

Yes | No = No duty

↓

Is it fair, just and reasonable to impose a duty?

↓

Yes | No = No duty

↓

Duty owed

Right branch:

No. Use **Alcock** rules

↓

Does the C have close ties to the victim?

↓ ↓

Yes | No

↓ ↓

Was C at the scene or its aftermath? | No duty owed

↓ → No

Yes | No duty owed

↓

Did the C witness events? → No

↓

Yes

↓

Duty owed | **No duty owed**

Self-test Questions on psychiatric harm

Which case highlighted the distinction between primary and secondary victims? Explain these 2 terms

In which case (in the HL) was the first successful claim for nervous shock by a secondary victim?

In that case what did the Lords say needed to be looked at in such claims?

*What was added in **Alcock v CC of South Yorkshire**?*

A general guide to revision

The first and foremost rule for revision is to start early. Too many students leave it until the last minute and then get in a panic. If you take it gently and organise your time properly you will feel a lot more calm and confident when exam time comes. Make a plan of what you want to cover each day and try to stick to it. Don't forget to include some breaks in your schedule, if you are tired it will be harder to retain the material you have been revising.

Here are a few tips for revision techniques

> *Go through your notes and try to summarise them*
>
> *Learn the key cases, as these are essential to know*
>
> *Make sure you understand how the judge has applied the law to the facts so you can do the same in an examination scenario*
>
> *For those of you who need to evaluate the law, if the case is one you may also want to use in an essay, be sure you understand any problems it raises or solves*
>
> *Go through the summaries of the topic. These provide the essential points which may need to be addressed*
>
> *Go to the examination board's website for past exam papers, mark schemes and reports*
>
> *Practice answering questions then look at the examiners' mark schemes and reports to see if you were on the right track*

Revision of duty, breach and causation for all types of loss

Proving a duty of care is the first step in any negligence claim. The rules for proving a duty will depend on whether the harm caused is physical, economic or psychiatric. The main difference between proving a duty for the three types of harm is proximity, it is needed for all three but the rules are stricter where the harm is not physical.

Physical harm – there must be proximity between C & D. This includes not only physical proximity but also the *relationship* between the parties. In **Bourhill v Young** she did not have sufficient proximity to the accident or to the driver so the claimed failed. In **Donoghue v Stevenson** the relationship between a manufacture and consumer was sufficient so the claim succeeded.

Economic loss – there must be a *special relationship* (between C & D). There was no such relationship in **Caparo v Dickman** so the claimed failed.

Psychiatric harm – there must be a *family* relationship or close ties (between C & V). There was no such relationship in **White v CC of South Yorkshire** so the claimed failed.

Summary diagram of duty for all types of loss

Type of Harm / Loss			
Physical (to person or property)	Psychiatric	Economic	
		By statement	By act
Duty based on **Donoghue / Caparo** test	Duty based on **Alcock** test	Duty based on **Hedley** test, **Caparo** test and assumption of responsibility	No duty
Go on to prove breach and causation	Go on to prove breach and causation	Go on to prove breach and causation	No claim

Task 13

Look up the tests mentioned above. Draw a diagram adding the tests for each type of harm or damage. Keep this for revision.

Breach of duty and causation are important factors for all types of loss. The rules on both these are the same whether the harm is physical, economic or psychiatric.

Breach of duty

The standard expected of D is that of the reasonable person, an objective test. Note, though the subjective element:

> *Bolam v Friern HMC/Bolitho v City & Hackney HA – the medical profession and other professionals*
>
> *Nettleship v Weston- learners*
>
> *Mullin v Richards- children*

There are four main factors to balance against each other in deciding what is reasonable:

> *the magnitude of risk – how likely is it that harm will occur? Bolton v Stone/Maguire v Harland & Wolff plc 2005*
>
> *the gravity of the potential harm – how much harm might occur? Paris v Stepney BC 1951*
>
> *whether the risk was justifiable – is the risk of harm a benefit to society in some way? Watt v Hertfordshire CC 1954*
>
> *the expense and practicality of taking precautions – how easy is it to avoid the harm occurring? Latimer v AEC 1952*

Summary

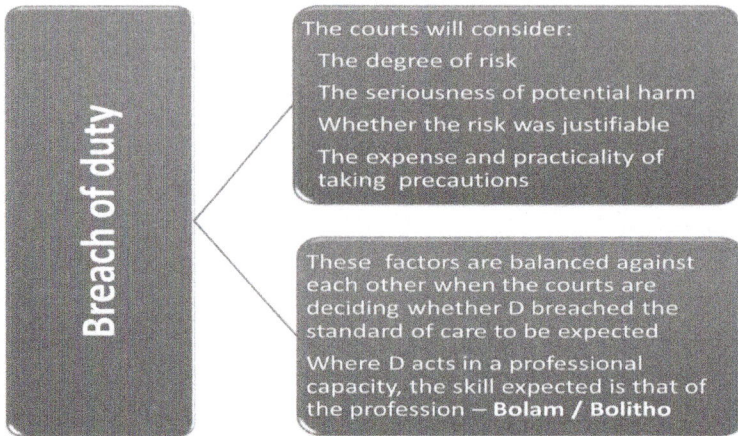

Breach of duty

The courts will consider:
The degree of risk
The seriousness of potential harm
Whether the risk was justifiable
The expense and practicality of taking precautions

These factors are balanced against each other when the courts are deciding whether D breached the standard of care to be expected
Where D acts in a professional capacity, the skill expected is that of the profession — **Bolam / Bolitho**

Damage caused by the breach

Causation must be proved both in fact and in law. If D's act or omission did not cause the harm there is no liability. This means considering the following questions:

Would the harm have occurred 'but for' D's act or omission? Barnett v Chelsea & Kensington HMC but note also Fairchild v Glenhaven Funeral Services Ltd

Was the harm foreseeable or was it too remote? The Wagon Mound

Was this type of harm foreseeable? Hughes v Lord Advocate

Does the thin-skull rule apply? Smith v Leech Brain

Summary

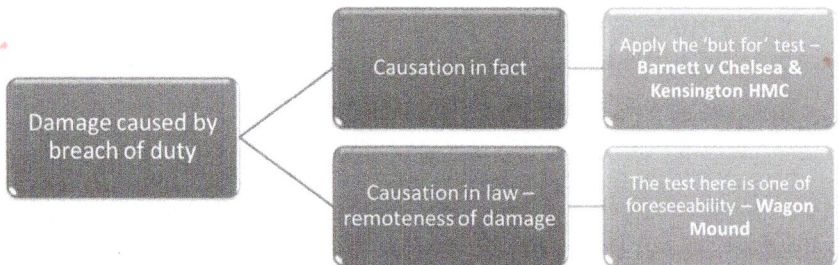

Damage caused by breach of duty

Causation in fact — Apply the 'but for' test — **Barnett v Chelsea & Kensington HMC**

Causation in law — remoteness of damage — The test here is one of foreseeability — **Wagon Mound**

Note that foreseeability comes into all 3 areas, but becomes more specific at each stage.

Duty	was it foreseeable that someone *could be* harmed by D's actions? **Donoghue**
Breach	was the *risk* of harm foreseeable? **Roe**
Causation	was this *type* of harm foreseeable? **The Wagon Mound / Hughes/Jolley**

Economic loss

Economic loss occurs in most claims. Where physical harm has been caused C may also suffer a loss which can be described in monetary terms such as damage to a car or loss of earnings. This can be claimed along with the claim for the physical harm caused; it is only **pure economic loss** which is limited. This is a loss which is ONLY financial and does not relate to any physical loss. A claim for pure economic loss will fail if it is the result of an act but may succeed in certain circumstances if it is the result of a **negligent misstatement**.

A statement would include something like a report, survey or reference. Things like this, especially if in the public domain, could be seen by millions and could 'open the floodgates' to litigation, therefore the rules on duty are more restrictive, mainly in relation to the 'proximity' issue.

Proximity is essentially a matter of finding a special relationship, and this involves the following:

D possesses a special skill

C reasonably relies on the statement

D knows that C is 'highly likely' to rely on the statement

It may also be necessary to consider the 'assumption of responsibility' and that any extension of liability should be incremental.

Task 14

Plans for a property had been done negligently and because of these plans the property was poorly built. Several defects appeared and the owner of the house, Nina, wants to claim for the reduction in value of the house due to these defects. As the plans had been done by the local council's building engineers she sues the council.

Do the council owe her a duty of care?

Would your answer differ if the defects led to a wall collapsing?

Task 15

Note down the cases from which the following principles come.

For negligent statements loss is claimable if there is a special relationship

Only loss related to physical damage is claimable for actions, not pure economic loss

A duty can be extended to a 3ʳᵈ party, e.g., a beneficiary of a will

A duty is not usually owed for social matters but may be if D has a particular skill that C relies on

If D knew that the statement would be relied on and had implied that they had expertise a duty will arise

There will only be a duty to a 3ʳᵈ party if it was "highly likely" C would rely on the statement

The duty owed to 3ʳᵈ parties can be extended to cases where the advice was not given to C but was about C

Psychiatric harm

The rules on cases of psychiatric harm were laid down in **McLoughlin v O'Brien** and restated by the HL in **Alcock v CC of South Yorkshire 1991**. They are called 'control mechanisms' as they control who can claim. C must have close ties of love and affection with the victim, there must be proximity to the incident or its immediate aftermath (proximity in time and space) and a sudden shock must have occurred which caused a recognisable psychiatric illness.

Before applying the control mechanisms the court must decide whether C is a primary or secondary victim. The court will also consider whether harm was foreseeable in a person of 'normal fortitude' (**Page v Smith**).

In the case of rescuers C may be either a primary or a secondary victim depending on the circumstances. The courts will look at whether the rescuer is in danger of harm, as stated in **White v CC of South Yorkshire**. In **White** and in **McFarlane v Caledonia Ltd** the rescuers were not in danger so were secondary victims, the claims therefore failed as the control mechanisms were not satisfied. In **McFarlane**, the court also held that C must be compared to a "person of ordinary fortitude", thus if C is particularly susceptible the claim could fail as long as an 'ordinary' person would not be likely to suffer psychiatric harm as a result of the events, as in **Monk v Harrington**. In **Page v Smith** the court again held that, in the case of secondary victims, only foreseeability of *psychiatric* harm, in a *'person of normal fortitude'*, will suffice. In this case C was in danger of harm so was a primary victim, the control mechanisms are not needed for primary victims so he merely had to prove a duty under **Caparo v Dickman**. Had he not been in danger of physical harm he would have to have shown that it was foreseeable that most people would have suffered psychiatric harm.

Task 16

Explain and apply the rules for secondary victims in cases of psychiatric harm to the facts of **Monk v Harrington 2008**. Conclude whether you think he succeeded in his claim, using cases in support.

Summary of the control mechanisms
The claimant must have a close tie of love and affection to a victim

> this will be presumed in the case of a parent, spouse or child of the victim, unless there is evidence to the contrary

> it could also extend to other relationships but in this case close ties must be proved by evidence

The claimant must be close to the event in time and space

> the claimant must be present at the scene (space and time) or its 'immediate aftermath' (time)

> this can include a visit to the mortuary but the visit must be connected to the event, so much may depend on any time gap between the event and the visit

The event must be perceived by the claimant

> it is not enough to be told about an event by a third party

> nor to witness events on television

> although a live broadcast may be different

Also the injury must be caused by a sudden shock, the shock must cause a recognisable psychiatric illness (supported by medical evidence) and it must be shown that a person of 'reasonable fortitude' would also have suffered psychiatric harm (i.e., *psychiatric* harm must be foreseeable).

Although different exam boards have different ways of styling their examination papers, there are always going to be common elements. You will need to be able to apply the law you have learnt to a particular scenario and for some boards you will need to be able to evaluate a given topic to provide a critique of the law, including reforms where appropriate. As not all examination boards require this it is dealt with in a separate section which can be omitted by those who do not need it (see '**Essay questions (evaluation)**').

A general guide to examination papers

Read **all** questions carefully before deciding which to answer

Look again at the ones you wish to answer to make sure you can do so, and make brief notes. This can be a useful checklist later when you are tired and your memory begins to fail.

Structure your answer. Remember this is a test of law so you need to state the legal principles involved and apply them to the particular question. A solid start is worth a lot and gets the examiner on your side. A small plan is helpful.

It is necessary to do more than regurgitate your notes. You need to be selective as to what is relevant, and to choose appropriate cases and examples in support of what you say.

Never put in irrelevant material just because you know it - there is **never** a question asking you to 'write all you know about...'. The examiner wants to know that you understand the specific issues and can apply the appropriate law to the facts given.

Always support your answer with **relevant** cases. Don't worry too much about the facts, the principle forming the *ratio decidendi* is usually the important part e.g. in **Donoghue v Stevenson** that you owe a duty to others to take care is vital but you don't need to write a paragraph discussing snails and ginger beer

Having said that, you want to show why you have chosen a particular case so will need to mention any facts that specifically relate to the scenario. If the scenario mentions someone being ill after consuming a chocolate bar with a dead mouse in it (yes, there has been a case!) then talking briefly about snails in ginger beer will be relevant. The main point here is that you need to be selective; this demonstrates a skill in itself and conserves precious time.

If you can't remember the name of a case that is relevant, don't leave it out but refer to it in a general way e.g. 'in one decided case....', 'in the case where there was a snail in a drink' or 'in a similar case....'

In problem questions, identify the various issues in the first paragraph and then set about dealing with them one by one, applying the relevant law to each issue, **referring to the facts of the question as you do so**. Referring to the specific facts in the question not only tells the examiner that you are answering the particular points raised but also failure to do this is a common complaint seen in examiners' reports. A short summing up is also a good idea e.g., "In conclusion it would appear that D may be liable for ... but it is possible that the defence of ... applies which will reduce/negate liability"

Finally, make sure you cover the whole question; there are only a certain number of marks available. The examiner has a mark scheme to work to, so however brilliant your answer to one part of the question is, missing out the other parts will severely reduce your total marks.

Examination practice for this topic

Problem scenarios (application)

There is limited time in most exams and examiners rarely set a question which requires you to cover everything. Application of the law requires you to be selective. The facts should point you to particular issues which need addressing and you must be prepared to pick out the relevant law and cases and to leave out anything irrelevant – for which you will gain no marks. To practice 'clue-spotting' do the following exercise.

Task 17: Application practice – clue-spotting

Look at the brief comments taken from problem scenarios and add what they indicate is the focus of the question. The first one is done for you as an example.

Tom's mother gave him a washing machine which broke down and damaged his clothes: *This indicates an action under the **CPA** is the focus because he did not buy the machine but it is defective. However if his clothes are worth less than £275 the **CPA** does not apply so consider negligence under **Donoghue v Stevenson/Caparo v Dickman***

Doctor Patel made an error of judgment and the patient suffered a stroke

The company spent a lot of money installing safety measures but Bob the boiler-man was injured when an electrical fault occurred

When responding to an emergency call with its siren blaring, the ambulance crashed into a car, seriously injuring the driver

In all problem questions, you need to take a logical approach. First, read the facts carefully to ensure that you understand the points raised by the scenario. Then apply the relevant law in a logical manner, using cases in support. There are several application practice tasks below so complete these and then do the examination question in full.

Examination tip

It is **good practice** to be selective. Select only the law that applies to the given facts. This shows that you understand the law well enough to know what is relevant.

It is **bad practice** to write all you know about an area just because you know it well. Even if it is right, you will gain no marks if it is not relevant to the facts given

All exam questions can be approached in a similar way;

   identify the law

   state the law (using relevant cases/statutes)

   apply the law (using relevant cases)

   reach a conclusion (based on your application)

Task 18: Application practice

As with the last exercise it is useful to practice 'clue-spotting'. Look at the following phrases which all relate to negligence of some kind. In each case either economic loss or psychiatric harm has occurred. Note any particular issues that the phrases bring to mind, with a relevant case (there may be more than one possibility). The first is done for you in italics.

He wasn't an expert but he implied that he was.

*This statement points to the need for D to possess a special skill. This can include where D implies he has a skill - **Esso Petroleum v Marden***

Tim produced a survey for the Building Society, but the couple buying the house...

He told her at the party that the shares were really good but...

The auditors were aware that a bid had been made for the company

Tom's employer was negligent when writing his reference

He was badly injured and his colleague saw it from an adjoining room

He saw it from a distance

Sue wasn't hurt but suffered shock at being involved in the accident

She rushed to the scene to find her daughter lying in the road

Pete ran to help

Task 19: Application practice

Jemima's daughter was missing and Jemima went out to look for her. She saw a police cordon around a car crash and believed her daughter was involved in the accident. She did not actually see who was involved though, as the body had already been taken to the mortuary, but the police told her it was a young girl. She immediately went to the mortuary and recognised that the girl's body was her daughter. She suffers psychiatric harm and claims against the negligent driver. Discuss the driver's liability for the harm caused to Jemima.

Examination tip

In a given scenario there will often be more than one possible C. Look for clues as to whether they are a primary or secondary V, e.g., is there an indication that a person is at risk of harm? For a primary victim you must apply the normal **Caparo** test, for a secondary victim the control mechanisms will need to be applied (and there could be both in one scenario). Take each person in turn and refer to the material in the scenario as you work through, remembering to use cases in support. When discussing the second (or third or fourth) person you needn't repeat everything, refer back to what you said before, but be careful to ensure the law applies in the same way.

Bearing in mind the advice given above, complete the following task.

Task 20: Application practice

Danny takes a bend too fast and crashes into another car. The other driver is killed and a passenger seriously injured. Sue hears the crash from her kitchen and goes into shock. Pete was cycling nearby and only narrowly missed being hit himself. He suffers black-outs afterwards. Ali stops at the lay-by opposite and rings for an ambulance, he is particularly prone to depression and suffers from acute depression afterwards. Tim passes in his car shortly afterwards and stops to give first aid. He is traumatised by the events. Explain whether Sue, Pete, Ali and Tim can claim against Danny.

Task 21: Examination practice – do this one in full

Andy writes an article in a magazine called 'Stocks and Shares' praising the company Megapixel and recommending that people should buy their shares. This magazine is well known and respected in the financial sector for the accuracy of its articles. Sven sees the article and invests in the shares but it turns out that Andy knows nothing about shares and the information is widely inaccurate. Sven loses several thousand pounds and sues Andy for making a negligent misstatement.

Martin and a friend found an old rotten boat on land owned by the council. While playing on the boat it collapsed and Martin was seriously injured. Angie, who was a neighbour of Martin and his family heard the screaming and ran to the scene. She called an ambulance and then rang Maria, Martin's mother, at work to tell her what had happened. The ambulance arrived and Angie saw Martin being carried on a stretcher covered in blood. The ambulance left and shortly afterwards Maria arrived at the scene. Both Maria and Angie later suffered from post-traumatic stress.

1. Consider what rights and remedies Sven has against Andy in connection with his loss

2. Consider what rights and remedies Angie and Maria might have against the council in connection with the harm they suffered

Essay questions (evaluation) – not all examination boards have essay questions but for those of you who need to evaluate the law here is a short general guide followed by some specific issues with this area of law.

In essay questions, you will usually be asked to form an opinion or to weigh up arguments for and against a particular statement. Here a broader range of knowledge is needed showing arguments for, arguments against and an evaluation of these arguments. If reforms have been proposed or implemented, discuss these too. You should always round off your answer with a short concluding paragraph, preferably using some of the wording from the question to indicate to the examiner that you are addressing the specific issue raised.

Essays should have a logical structure. The beginning, should introduce the subject matter, the central part should explain/analyse/criticise it as appropriate, and the conclusion should bring the various strands of argument together with reference to the question set.

Try to consider alternative arguments. A well-rounded essay will bring in other views even if you disagree with them; you cannot shoot them down without setting them up first.

Essay writing is a skill in itself, so here is a brief guide on how to structure your essay.

Writing a discussion essay: staging the information logically

If you stage your essay as follows, it will make it easy to read, logically structured and easier to write. It may also mean you don't leave out important points. Here's how it works:

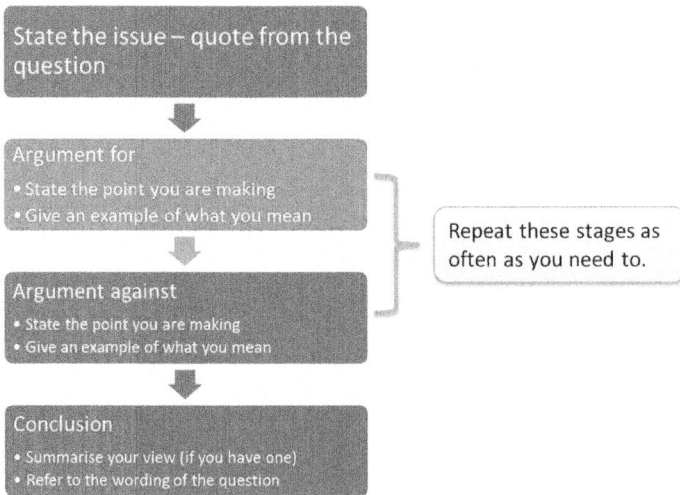

State the issue – quote from the question

Argument for
• State the point you are making
• Give an example of what you mean

Argument against
• State the point you are making
• Give an example of what you mean

Repeat these stages as often as you need to.

Conclusion
• Summarise your view (if you have one)
• Refer to the wording of the question

Finally, make sure you cover the whole question. For both problem and evaluation questions, there are only a certain number of marks available. The examiner has a mark scheme to work to, so however brilliant your answer to one part of the question is, missing out the other parts will severely reduce your total marks.

These are examples of an examination question from each area, economic loss and psychiatric harm.

Economic loss: *The law on negligent misstatement is complex and unpredictable and needs reforming.*

Discuss the accuracy of this statement.

Psychiatric harm: Judges have imposed strict limitations on who can claim for psychiatric harm because it is recognised that many people can be affected by disasters such as that seen in Alcock.

Discuss the accuracy of this statement.

A logical approach is needed for essay questions as well as problem questions. You should:

State what the current law is

Identify and explain where it is unsatisfactory

Support your comments with cases and/or examples

Discuss where reforms are needed including any that have been proposed or implemented

There is no 'right' answer to evaluation questions, opinions vary and you can form your own - but **always** use cases and/or examples to back up what you say. There are several criticisms that can be made about the law in these areas which could be discussed in an essay.

Key criticisms include:

The Caparo test includes looking at policy issues, usually a matter for an elected government and Parliament

On the other hand there is a need for a balance to be struck between certainty and flexibility. People need to know what the law is so that it can be relied on, but at the same time the law may need to adapt to the circumstances

Making a distinction between economic loss by actions and by statements seems illogical. There is little difference between the solicitor's negligence in White v Jones and that of the building inspector approving the plans in Murphy. It could be argued that as long as the Caparo test is satisfied a duty could be imposed whatever the type of loss. Any need for restricting the rules in cases where many people may have claims could be dealt with within the 'fair, just and reasonable' part of the test

Should children be able to sue the council for failing to e.g., diagnose dyslexia as in Phelps v Hillingdon BC or special needs as in Carty? Would the money be better used in employing more (and better) psychologists?

It can be argued that a duty should not have been owed in Chaudhry v Prabhakar as imposing a duty in a social situation could make people reluctant to help out a friend

It may be difficult to prove 'close ties' in psychiatric harm cases where it is not a family relationship. Extending the relationship from the immediate family to those with close ties in Alcock v CC of South Yorkshire seems fair. A loving relationship with a partner may be much closer than one between a husband and wife who have grown apart. The problem is how you prove 'close ties'. It is presumed in cases of spouse and parents but what about brothers, uncles, grandparents and friends – all of whom failed in Alcock? The Law Commission proposes that the 'close ties' requirement should be kept, albeit with some extension of the presumptions

The 'immediate aftermath' is hard to measure and cases are not always consistent (Alcock/Atkinson)

The law has not been entirely consistent on several of the issues involving psychiatric harm. The implication in Alcock was that 'sudden shock' would not include any illness caused by, for example, long-term caring for a terminally ill relative. However Walters shows that this requirement may have been relaxed. Secondly, it has been made clear that 'normal grief' is not enough. However, the father succeeded in Vernon v Bosley because the 'abnormal' grief could not be distinguished from the 'normal grief' to be expected. It may be hard to decide what is 'normal' because what is normal in one person may be abnormal in another.

Task 1

You may have put it slightly differently but one way of putting it would be that you should take care not to do something, or fail to do something, that might harm others. This does not mean everyone but those who are likely to be affected by your actions, e.g., people you should have considered before acting or omitting to act. Applying this to **Donoghue v Stevenson**, a manufacturer should owe a duty to a consumer because a consumer is someone likely to be affected by the actions and omissions of a manufacturer. A consumer is also someone whom a manufacturer ought to have in mind when manufacturing the product, in this case ginger beer.

Task 2

Mrs D couldn't sue the shopkeeper because she had no contract with the shopkeeper, her friend bought the drink.

She sued the manufacturer and the HL decided that a manufacturer owes a duty to the consumer.

A better action now would be under the **Consumer Protection Act** as she would not have to prove breach of duty, merely that there was a defect which caused damage or harm.

Applying the **Consumer Protection Act**, Mrs Donoghue would have to show that the manufacturer (Stevenson) was the producer and that the product was defective. A manufacturer of products such as ginger beer is a producer under **s 2**. **S 1** applies to all goods and electricity so the ginger beer will come within this. **S 3** provides that there is a defect if the safety of the product is not what should be expected by people in general, taking account of such things as warnings and how the product was used. This seems to indicate there was a defect as most people would not expect a snail in their drink. Also there was no evidence of any warning that the beer 'could contain snails'! She would not need to prove a breach of duty as liability is strict, and the snail in the beer caused personal injury, so she would succeed in a claim under the **Act**.

Self-test questions on duty

In **Sutherland Shire County v Heyman**, Brennan J said

"It is preferable, in my view, that the law should develop novel categories of negligence incrementally and by analogy with established categories."

The three-part **Caparo** test is:

there must be foreseeability of harm

there must be proximity between C and D

it must be fair, just and reasonable to impose a duty on D

Among others, police, hospitals, rescue services and local councils might be immune from owing a duty.

No duty was owed in **Bourhill v Young** because there was no proximity between her and the driver because she was not at the scene.

No duty was owed in **Caparo v Dickman** because there was no proximity between the investor and the auditors, nor was it fair, just and reasonable to impose a duty.

Task 3

Bolton v Stone - the cricket club owed a duty to passers-by

Paris v Stepney BC - the employer owed a duty to the employee

Watt v Hertfordshire CC - the council (or employer) owed a duty to the employee

Latimer v AEC - the employer owed a duty to the employee

Nettleship v Weston - the learner driver owed a duty to her driving instructor

Mullin v Richards school - pupils owed a duty to each other

Bolam v Friern HMC - the doctor owed a duty to the patient

McDonnell v Holwerda - the doctor (or general practitioner) owed a duty to the patient

Vowles v Evans – the referee owed a duty to the players

Task 4

You may have chosen others cases, but here is one example. In **The Scout Association v Mark Barnes 2010**, the important factor was whether the activity had sufficient social value to be justified. The CA thought the value was limited and therefore the risk was not justified. Applying the other factors, it can be said that the risk of harm was foreseeable because the main lights were off and the scouts were running around in the semi-dark. The seriousness of harm would not seem that great though, because there is only a limited amount of harm that can be caused by people running around indoors. The club had taken some precautions by using the emergency lighting but arguably should have removed the furniture, at least at floor level. On balance although the gravity of the potential harm was low the other factors would come done on the side of breach. The risk was foreseeable, only minimum precautions were taken, and the lack of social value would be a deciding factor in finding the Scout Association had breached its duty.

Task 5

Here is an simple diagram with some cases added.

- Reasonable parent (**Harris v Perry**)
- Reasonable employer (**Daw v Intel**)
- Reasonable child (**Mullins/Orchard v Lee**)
- Reasonable doctor (**Bolam/Bolitho**)

The standard expected is based on 4 factors:

- The degree of risk (**Bolton v Stone**)
- The seriousness of potential harm (**Paris v Stepney BC**)
- Whether the risk was justifiable (**Watts**)
- The expense and practicality of taking precautions (**Latimer**)

Self-test questions on breach

The objective standard was explained by Baron Alderson in **Blyth v Birmingham Waterworks Co. 1856**

The standard expected of a professional is the standard of a person in that line of work

The standard expected of a child is the standard of a child of similar age, not an adult

The employers had not breached their duty in **Maguire v Harland & Wolff plc (2005)** because at the time of C's exposure the risks of secondary exposure were unknown. The injury to a member of C's family was therefore not foreseeable

Task 6

The answer depends on your chosen cases but here is one example from the duty cases and one from breach.

In **Watson v British Boxing Board 2000**, the boxer Michael Watson suffered head injuries during a fight against Chris Eubank. He sued the Board on the basis that had proper medical treatment been given at the ringside he would not have suffered brain damage. It can be said that 'but for' the failure to provide medical treatment he would not have suffered brain damage. As regards remoteness of damage, it is foreseeable that if medical treatment is not available at a boxing match where people are hitting each other, then someone could suffer harm. As harm is foreseeable it is not too remote from the negligent act or omission (the failure to provide medical treatment) so the **Wagon Mound** test is also satisfied.

In **Palmer v Cornwall CC 2009**, a boy of 14 hit another boy in the eye while throwing stones at seagulls. The CA held that only one supervisor for around 300 children was clearly inadequate so the council was in breach of duty. It can be said that 'but for' this breach the boy would not have been injured. It is also foreseeable that if there is not adequate supervision the boys may do something like this (based on the idea that children are likely to "do the unexpected" as held in **Jolley**). The harm was therefore not too remote from the breach of duty (the failure to provide adequate supervision).

Task 7

Duty: Applying the **Caparo** test to the facts of **Barnett v Kensington & Chelsea HMC**, the doctor owed a duty because it is foreseeable that a hospital's actions could cause harm to patients coming to casualty. There is a relationship between a hospital doctor and an outpatient so there is sufficient proximity. Although the hospital is a public authority (and so arguably there are policy reasons not to impose a duty), in these circumstances it is most likely to be fair, just and reasonable to impose a duty of care as a hospital should care for those who are ill. There is no 'floodgates' issue because the duty is limited to patients and not the public in general (thus it is more likely **Reeves v MPC** will be followed, rather than **Hill**).

Breach: The doctor breached his duty as he has not reached the standard of a reasonable doctor. A doctor is judged against those in the same profession so if medical opinion shows it would be more usual to at least examine the patient there will be a breach (**Bolam v Friern HMC**). This medical opinion must have some logical basis (**Bolitho v City & Hackney HA**) but that would seem to be the case as it is normal to examine patients. The courts balance several factors in deciding what is reasonable. These include how big the risk is, what harm might occur from taking the risk, whether the risk is justified and how practical it would be to avoid the risk. There is quite a high risk of harm because no examination at all took place so in these circumstances harm is foreseeable. The potential harm is relatively serious as he could have had any number of serious ailments which might have been picked up in an examination. There could be a public benefit in not using up valuable resources but this is unlikely to be persuasive as it is minimal in relation to the other factors. Where the risk of harm is high, there is a greater obligation to take sufficient precautions to avoid it. Here this would only require minimal precautions, just doing the examination, so it is not impractical to expect more care to be taken. In **Barnett v Chelsea & Kensington HMC**, on balance, the doctor did not act as a reasonable doctor would have done.

Causation: The doctor owed a duty which he breached, so the remaining issue is whether the breach caused the man's death. Causation has to be proved BOTH in fact and in law. Here causation in fact is not proved because the harm would have occurred anyway. The answer to the question 'but for the breach of duty would he have died?' is 'yes', the evidence showed that he would have died anyway, so the doctor's breach did not cause the death. As causation in fact is not proved there is no need to consider causation in law.

Self-test questions on causation

The 'but for' test asks 'but for D's action would harm have occurred? It comes from **Barnett v Chelsea & Kensington HMC**

The Wagon Mound case established the rule on foreseeability

Hughes added that if the *type* of harm is foreseeable this is enough; the exact harm need not be

The 'thin skull rule' means that if a person is harmed because he/she is particularly vulnerable (e.g., has a thin skull), D is liable for the full consequences even if someone without the vulnerability would not have been harmed to the same degree.

The point made in **Jolley v Sutton LBC** (in the HL) in regard to children, was that they do the unexpected

Task 8

In **JEB Fasteners Ltd v Mark Bloom 1983**, the auditors prepared company accounts knowing that anyone considering a takeover would rely on the accounts. This differs from **Caparo** where the auditors did not know that potential shareholders would rely on the accounts and also they were not done for the purpose of informing shareholders but for the company. There was therefore not enough proximity to satisfy the special relationship requirement

Task 9

Applying the rules on special relationship to the facts of **Smith v Bush**, the surveyor clearly possessed a special skill. The surveyor also knew who would use the information and for what purpose because although he was employed by the mortgage lender, he knew the report would be passed to the buyers, who would be 'highly likely' to rely on it for the purpose of deciding whether to buy the house. Finally, as stated by the HL in the case, it was reasonable for them to rely on it. This was partly because the use and purpose were known, and also because it was unrealistic to expect the buyer to get their own survey done as well as having to pay for the building society one. As regards whether he voluntarily assumed responsibility, this is less clear, but in most professional cases it can be said that a person would voluntarily assume responsibility for information given which relates to that profession (an accountant for accounts, a solicitor for drawing up a will, as in **White v Jones**, a surveyor for a property report etc.).

Self-test questions on economic loss

A special relationship exists where.

> *A special skill is possessed by D, who makes the statement*
>
> *C reasonably relies on D's statement*
>
> *D knows that C is 'highly likely' to rely on the statement*

The claim failed in the **Mutual Life** case because the advice was outside D's area of expertise

Smith v Bush shows a surveyor may not owe a duty to a buyer in a commercial transaction

The above case was distinguished in **Scullion v Bank of Scotland plc 2011**

In **White v Jones**, the emphasis was on the assumption of responsibility by a professional

Longmore LJ summarised the position in **Customs and Excise Commissioners v Barclays Bank** by saying that in cases of economic loss it was appropriate to use each of the following tests:

> *the 3-fold Caparo test:*
>> *foreseeability*
>> *proximity*
>> *whether it is fair, just and reasonable to impose a duty*
> *the 'assumption of responsibility' test*
> *the 'incremental' test*

Task 10
The main difference was that in **Hambrook** the mother not only had a close relationship, she had also seen the incident and shock was foreseeable.

Task 11
The difference between the passenger in **Page v Smith** and the police in **White v CC of South Yorkshire** was that the passenger in **Page** was in danger himself and so a primary victim. The police claims failed because they were classed as secondary victims and so had to satisfy the control mechanisms. They could not do this as they had no relationship to any of the victims.

Task 12
This is only for those who will need to do essay questions in the examination. Look at the Key criticisms in the examination practice section.

Self-test questions on psychiatric harm
Page v Smith highlighted the distinction between primary and secondary victims

A primary victim is in foreseeable danger of harm, whereas a secondary victim is not directly affected but witnesses the event. The distinction is important because if C is a primary victim there is no need to apply the control mechanisms; the **Caparo** test applies as for physical harm

McLoughlin v O'Brien was the first successful claim for nervous shock by a secondary victim (in the HL)

The Lords said the following needed to be looked at in such claims:

the relationship between C and the victim

the proximity of C to the accident

the means by which the shock was caused

Alcock v CC of South Yorkshire added that there must be a sudden shock which causes a recognisable psychiatric illness

Task 13

You should have added the following in your diagram:

Physical harm (Caparo v Dickman): Foreseeability, proximity and whether it is fair, just and reasonable to impose a duty

Economic loss (Hedley Byrne v Heller): There must be a special relationship which involves:

D possesses a special skill

C reasonably relies on D's statement

D knows that C is 'highly likely' to rely on the statement

Psychiatric harm (Alcock v CC of South Yorkshire): C must have close ties of love and affection with the victim, have been present at the scene or its immediate aftermath and there must be a sudden shock

Task 14

It is unlikely that the council owe Nina a duty of care because pure economic loss is not usually recoverable. This situation is comparable to the case of **Murphy v Brentwood DC.** In **Murphy** the HL held that there was no duty in similar circumstances. The loss in value of the property was purely economic; no actual damage had been caused so the claim failed.

If the defects actually caused damage any loss would be recoverable as the loss in value would then be a result of physical damage. This is *consequential* economic loss so the usual rules for physical harm would apply.

Task 15

For negligent statements loss is claimable if there is a special relationship - **Hedley Byrne v Heller**

Only loss related to physical damage is claimable for actions, not pure economic loss - **Spartan Steel and Alloys Ltd v Martin & Co**

A duty can be extended to a 3rd party, e.g., a beneficiary of a will - **White v Jones**

A duty is not usually owed for social matters but may be if D has a particular skill that C relies on - **Chaudhray v Prabhakar**

If D knew that the statement would be relied on and had implied that they had expertise a duty will arise - **Esso Petroleum v Marden**

There will only be a duty to a 3rd party if it was "highly likely" C would rely on the statement - **Smith v Bush**

The duty owed to 3rd parties can be extended to cases where the advice was not given to C but was about C - **Spring v Guardian Assurance plc**

Task 16

Applying the control mechanisms to the facts in **Monk v Harrington** it appears that C had no relationship to the victims as this usually applies to family members, or at least to those with whom C has close ties of love and affection, as stated in **Alcock v CC of South Yorkshire**. This is unlikely in this situation as he appears not to have known the victims. He was arguably in close proximity to the accident, although he was not at the scene he went there to help. It does not say how long after the incident this was but in **McLoughlin v O'Brien** it was enough to arrive in the 'immediate aftermath' and in **Taylorson v Shieldness** this aftermath extended to two days. Applying the rules on rescuers, it has been made clear (in **White v CC of South Yorkshire** and in **McFarlane v Caledonia Ltd**) that unless in danger themselves rescuers are secondary victims. Monk believed he was in danger but the court held that his belief was unreasonable in the circumstances (presumably there was evidence that he was not in danger) so it is likely that **McFarlane** would be followed. In **McFarlane** he was not in danger so his claim failed, the court also held that C must be compared to a "person of ordinary fortitude" and this was confirmed in **Page v Smith**. As Monk's belief that he was in danger was unreasonable it is unlikely that psychiatric harm was foreseeable, and secondly because he had this unreasonable belief he was probably not comparable to a person of normal fortitude. In conclusion his claim will fail as he cannot prove that he meets the criteria for secondary victims, so there will be no duty owed to him.

Task 17

Tom's mother gave him a washing machine which broke down and damaged his clothes: *This indicates an action under the **CPA** is the focus because he did not buy the machine but it is defective. However if his clothes are worth less than £275 the **CPA** does not apply so consider negligence under **Donoghue/Caparo***

The doctor made an error of judgment and the patient suffered a stroke: *This indicates the focus is the standard of care required of the medical profession. The **Bolam** test needs to be applied in such cases, as amended by **Bolitho v City & Hackney HA**. Thus Dr Patel must act in accordance with what would be normal practice in the opinion of a reasonable medical body, and that opinion must have a logical basis.*

The company spent a lot of money installing state-of-the-art safety measures but Bob the boiler-man was injured when an electrical fault occurred: *This indicates the focus is on the breach factors, in particular whether precautions against a risk have been taken and* whether expecting any more would be impractical, as in **Latimer v AEC**. It seems a lot has been done as the company spent 'a lot of money' and although spending money would not usually be enough alone, it would seem sufficient precautions have been taken as the safety measures are said to be 'state-of-the-art'.

When responding to an emergency call with its siren blaring, the ambulance crashed into a car, seriously injuring the driver: *This indicates that the breach factors are again the focus, here in particular whether the risk was justifiable. As the ambulance was reacting to an emergency this is likely to be the case, as in **Watt v Hertfordshire CC**. Also they had the 'siren blaring' so have taken precautions against the risk of harm.*

Task 18

He wasn't an expert but he implied that he was.

*This statement points to the need for D to possess a special skill. This can include where D implies he has a skill - **Esso Petroleum v Marden***

Tim produced a survey for the Building Society, but the couple buying the house...

*This points to the fact that there is not usually a duty to a third party, but may be if D knows that person will rely on the information - **Smith v Bush***

He told her at the party that the shares were really good but...

*The issue is that a social occasion will not usually lead to a duty for economic loss, however if he is a share expert and she knows this it may be reasonable for her to rely on the advice - **Chaudhray v Prabhakar***

The auditors were aware that a bid had been made for the company

*This indicates that a special relationship is more likely where D knows who will use the information - **JEB Fasteners Ltd v Mark Bloom / Law Society v KPMG Peat Marwick***

Tom's employer was negligent when writing his reference

*This indicates that although there is not usually a duty to a third party an exception is possible in the case of a reference where the information is about the other person - **Spring v Guardian Assurance plc***

He was badly injured and his colleague saw it from an adjoining room

*The focus is on proximity and as he was near in both time and space this is satisfied as it was an 'adjoining room' and seen first-hand. However a colleague is not in a presumed relationship so he needs to prove close ties to the victim - **McLoughlin v O'Brien/Alcock v CC of South Yorkshire***

He saw it from a distance

*Here he is likely to be seen as a bystander so proximity is not satisfied - **McFarlane v Caledonia Ltd***

Sue wasn't hurt but suffered shock at being involved in the accident

*The fact that Sue was 'involved in the accident' suggests that she was at risk of harm. Therefore she is a primary victim so does not have to satisfy the controls - **Page v Smith**. The ordinary rules under **Caparo v Dickman** apply to primary victims.*

She rushed to the scene to find her daughter lying in the road

*The issue is that proximity can include the 'immediate aftermath' so she would satisfy the proximity requirement for psychiatric harm and also as a mother is in a presumed relationship with the victim - **McLoughlin v O'Brien***

Pete ran to help

*Here Pete's role as a rescuer needs to be considered. He may be either a primary or secondary victim, if he is at risk of harm he is a primary victim but if he is not in danger the control mechanisms apply - **Chadwick v BTC / White v CC of South Yorkshire***

Task 19

Jemima will be a secondary victim as she was not in any danger, so as in **White v CC of South Yorkshire** she will need to satisfy the control mechanisms from **Alcock v CC of South Yorkshire**. As regards close ties of love and affection, these will be presumed in the case of a mother and child, as in **McLoughlin v O'Brien**. She also needs to establish proximity to the accident i.e., be at the scene or its immediate aftermath, and have seen it with her own senses. This may be more difficult because although she went to the scene at that time she did not know that her daughter was even involved, let alone been killed. She was told by the police a young girl was involved but she did not know it was her daughter and also the HL in **Alcock** said that being told by a third party was not enough. The time lapse will be relevant. In **Alcock**, visits to the mortuary several hours after the event were not sufficiently close to the incident to be considered the immediate aftermath. However, here she went to the mortuary 'immediately' so **Alcock** can be distinguished. If the visit to the mortuary was sufficiently connected to the events at the police cordon to come within the immediate aftermath Jemima may succeed in her claim, based on the decision in **McLoughlin v O'Brien**.

*N.B., these facts are based on **Atkinson v Seghal** where the court held that the mother was owed a duty of care.*

Task 20: Application practice

Taking each person in turn:

Sue is unlikely to prove Danny owes her a duty, like the woman in **Bourhill v Young**, she was not in close proximity to the events. A distinction was made in **Page v Smith** between primary and secondary victims. She is not in any danger so is a secondary victim and must satisfy the **Alcock v CC of South Yorkshire** control mechanisms. These are that she must be a witness to the event or the immediate aftermath and must have a close relationship or close ties of love and affection to the victim. There is no evidence of any relationship to a victim here so she will fail in her claim.

Pete will be a primary victim as he was 'cycling nearby' and at risk of being hit himself, therefore Danny will owe him a duty as long as he satisfies the normal tests for physical harm. Applying **Caparo v Dickman**, it is foreseeable that driving too fast can cause harm, he is in proximity to Danny as he 'only narrowly missed being hit' by him, and finally there are no policy reasons to suggest it will not be fair just and reasonable to impose a duty and doing so will not open the floodgates to other claims. As a duty is owed we need to go on to consider breach and causation. The duty has been breached as he has not acted as a reasonable competent driver (**Nettleship v Weston**). Balancing the various factors we can say that driving too fast round a bend has a high degree of risk (**Bolton v Stone**), the potential harm is serious as people can be killed by such actions (**Paris v Stepney BC**), the cost of preventing the risk would be nil as he only had to slow down, unlike in **Latimer v AEC** where it would have been impractical to do more, and finally there is no social benefit to his actions. The negligent driving has caused the harm in fact as 'but for' Danny's breach Pete would not have suffered harm (**Barnett v Chelsea & Kensington HMC**). Legal causation is also proved as the harm was foreseeable and therefore not too remote from the breach (**The Wagon Mound**). As long as some harm was foreseeable that is enough, the exact type does not have to be foreseeable (**Hughes**).

Ali is likely to be seen as a 'mere bystander' as in **McFarlane v Caledonia Ltd.** He is not in any danger himself, so again we need to apply the **Alcock v CC of South Yorkshire** rules. As with Sue above, he is not in close proximity to the events and there is no evidence of any relationship. He is also unlikely to be seen as a person of 'normal fortitude' as required by the courts in **Page v Smith** and **McFarlane v Caledonia Ltd** because he is 'particularly prone to depression'.

Tim will be classed as a rescuer and if **Chadwick v BTC** is followed he may be owed a duty. However the situation is different here because he is not in danger himself, so is more likely to be classed as a secondary victim, as in **White**. This means applying the **Alcock v CC of South Yorkshire** rules. He has proximity in time and space as 'shortly afterwards' is likely to be seen as the 'immediate aftermath' as in **McLoughlin v O'Brien**. However he has no relationship to the victims so, as in **White v CC of South Yorkshire**, although he has proximity his claim will fail – all the criteria must be met.

Task 21

1. Sven's loss is economic rather than physical and the rules for proving a duty are different in such cases. Although pure economic loss cannot usually be claimed, there is an exception where the loss is caused by a negligent misstatement, in this case the article.

In order to prove Andy owes him a duty of care, Sven will need to establish a special relationship with Andy as required by **Hedley Byrne v Heller**.

There are several element s to this. That D has a special skill or expertise, that D knows that C is relying on the statement and also that C reasonably relies on the statement. Where D knows the purpose for which the information will be used this will indicate the required knowledge, as in **JEB Fasteners Ltd v Mark Bloom** and **Law Society v KPMG Peat Marwick**. Another element in cases of economic loss is whether D voluntarily takes responsibility for the statement, as decided in **White v Jones**. In **Customs and Excise** the CA held that the tests overlapped and no one was paramount, although the court suggested that a voluntary assumption of responsibility could be enough alone and the HL approved the comments of the CA (although reversing the actual decision). It is not clear that Andy has voluntarily assumed responsibility for his article, particularly as there is not a specific person to whom he gave advice (unlike in **Phelps v Hillingdon BC** where there was a responsibility to a specific child). Therefore the test from **Hedley Byrne v Heller** should be applied.

Here Andy does not appear to have a special skill or expertise because he 'knows nothing about shares'. However, there could be an implied expertise because he is writing in a well-respected magazine and is holding himself out as being knowledgeable, as in **Esso Petroleum v Marden** and **Lennon v MPC**. If there is found to be an implied expertise then we need to consider whether Andy knew Sven would rely on the statement and whether it was reasonable for Sven to do so

Again, the fact that the magazine is well respected in the financial sector means that Andy will realise that readers will believe the advice and are 'highly likely' to rely on it. As in **JEB Fasteners Ltd v Mark Bloom** he knows the purpose for which the information will be used. In **JEB** the court did not require that D should be able to identify a particular individual who would rely on the information. It was enough that they knew someone would rely on it. If this was followed Andy may be liable.

Andy may argue that, as in **Caparo v Dickman**, there is not enough proximity for a special relationship to arise because the magazine may be read by anyone, so he does not know who will rely on his statement. However it is possible that **Caparo v Dickman** may be distinguished because here it is a magazine aimed at a particular audience, people interested in buying shares. Arguably there is a known purpose for using the information as the magazine is in the business of supplying exactly the information that Sven has relied on. The case of **Law Society v KPMG Peat Marwick** can support this as in that case there was liability because it was known that the information would be passed to the Law Society.

It seems reasonable for Sven to rely on the advice, again because it is a well-respected magazine aimed at a particular group of people.

On balance Andy may owe a duty of care to the readership of the magazine for his statement about the shares. As he knows nothing about shares it is not difficult to argue that he has breached his duty as there is a highly foreseeable risk that losses could be caused by his inaccurate advice and for the same reason the loss is not too remote so causation is proved.

If he succeeds the remedy will be an award of damages to put him in the position he would have been in had Andy not been negligent. This would be for the loss of the investments.

2. The harm suffered by both Angie and Maria is psychiatric so special rules apply when proving the council owe them a duty of care.

The first thing to consider is whether Angie and Maria were primary or secondary victims as decided in **Page v Smith**. As a primary victim is a person who is in danger of harm, and neither of them was in danger, nor in fear for their own safety, they will be secondary victims. This means applying the control mechanisms from **Alcock v CC of South Yorkshire**. The first of these is whether either of them have 'close ties of love and affection' to the victim, Martin. In the case of a parent such ties are presumed, as in **McLoughlin v O'Brien**, so Maria will satisfy this point. Angie may have a problem with this as she will have to provide evidence of such ties and this is unlikely to be the case as she is a neighbour. However, maybe it is possible she can provide the necessary evidence e.g., if she has known Martin all his life and frequently looks after him while Maria is at work. If this is the case she could succeed. The second issue is whether there was sufficient proximity in time and space and this means being at the scene or its 'immediate aftermath'. In this case it is Angie who is in the stronger position as she saw Martin 'covered in blood'. Maria did not arrive until the ambulance had left so will have more difficulty satisfying this part of the test. There is no evidence that she went to the hospital as was the case in **McLoughlin**, so unless there was evidence at the scene such as something belonging to Martin that was covered in blood, she is likely to fail on this point. The HL in **Alcock** also made clear that there must be a sudden shock and that the shock must cause a recognisable psychiatric illness, so medical evidence will be needed.

In both cases there is post-traumatic stress and this is a recognisable psychiatric illness so there should not be a problem in supplying medical evidence. It is not clear, however, whether either of them suffered a 'sudden' shock. This is more likely in respect of Angie as the sight of Martin covered in blood could have caused a sudden shock. It is less likely in the case of Maria as she did not see Martin and it was also made clear in **Alcock** that being told about events by a third party is not enough, so the telephone call would not suffice even if it caused a sudden shock.

Case law is not fully consistent on these issues, which overlap to some extent. In **Sion v Hampstead AHA**, a father who suffered psychiatric harm after watching his son deteriorate and die over a period of two weeks failed in his claim as his harm was not caused by a sudden shock. However, in **North Glamorgan NHST v Walters** a mother who suffered psychiatric harm after sitting with her 10-month old baby as his condition deteriorated, until his life support system was turned off a couple of days later, succeeded in her claim. The CA held that the 'sudden shock' requirement in **Alcock** had been satisfied. In **Atkinson v Seghal**, at the trial the court had held that the shock was caused by being told of her daughter's death by the police (a third party) and rejected the claim. The CA reversed this, but it was mainly because the woman had also visited the mortuary shortly afterwards, so her psychiatric harm was caused in part by this visit, not only by being told the news of her daughter's death by the police.

On balance Angie may succeed in her claim if she can provide evidence of close ties to Martin, but Maria is less likely to succeed as she did not witness either the events or the aftermath. Once a duty is proved it must be shown that the council breached it. This will not be difficult on these facts which are very close to those in **Jolley**, and as that was a decision of the House of Lords it is likely to be followed. Although the claimant here is not the boy himself, this will not affect the breach as the council should not have left the boat in such a dangerous state. A reasonable council would have removed it. As for causation, we can say but for the council leaving a rotten boat on their land no harm would have been caused to anyone so the breach factually caused the harm. It is foreseeable that someone may be injured but possibly not foreseeable that psychiatric harm will result, and it was made clear in **Page v Smith** that a secondary victim must prove foreseeability of psychiatric harm. It is therefore possible that even if duty and breach is proved the harm suffered may be too remote from that breach, and so legal causation will not be present.

If either claim should succeed despite these issues then the remedy will be monetary damages to compensate for the harm caused and any relevant expenses.

Appendix: Abbreviations and acknowledgements

The following abbreviations are commonly used. You may use them in an examination answer, but write them in full the first time, e.g., write 'actual bodily harm (ABH)' and then after that you can just write 'ABH'.

General

Draft Code – A Criminal Code for England and Wales (Law Commission No. 177), 1989

CCRC Criminal Cases Review Commission

ABH actual bodily harm

GBH grievous bodily harm

D defendant

C claimant

V Victim

CA Court of Appeal

HL House of Lords

SC Supreme Court

Acts

S – Section (thus **s 1** Theft Act 1968 refers to section 1 of that Act)

s 1(2) means section 1 subsection 2 of an Act.

OAPA – Offences against the Person Act 1861

In cases – these don't need to be written in full

CC (at beginning) chief constable

CC (at end) county council

BC borough council

DC district council

LBC London borough council

AHA Area Health Authority

J Justice

LJ Lord Justice

LCJ Lord Chief Justice

LC Lord Chancellor

AG Attorney General

CPS Crown Prosecution Service

DPP Director of Public Prosecutions

AG Attorney General

.

Printed in Great Britain
by Amazon

18660129R00051